A Visual Guide to Chords and Arpeggios for Plectrum Banjo in CGBD

Benjamin M. Taylor

Contents

11

"Music creates order out of chaos: for rhythm imposes unanimity upon the divergent, melody imposes continuity upon the disjointed, and harmony imposes compatibility upon the incongruous." *Yehudi Menuhin.*

A carefully planned harmony (i.e. sequence of chords) can indeed profoundly affect the way a melody line is interpreted: my favourite example is 'The Swan' by Saint Saens. By presenting you with full fingerboard diagrams for each chord/arpeggio, the aims of this book are (i) to help you to construct original-sounding chordal accompaniment by considering non-standard fingerings and (ii) to help you visualise the pattern of notes in each arpeggio. The idea is for you to learn to recognise all the possible ways you could play a chord or an arpeggio in any key. Full fingerboard diagrams are advantageous because they allow you to pick out quirky fingerings: unusual ways of executing a chord that can make your music sound unique (for example the use of open strings).

How to Use This Book

Figure 1 below shows two example chords from this book: on the left are the notes of a C major chord and on the right are the notes of a C13sus4 chord; there are three different tones in the former (C E G) and six in the latter (C F G B D (F) A).

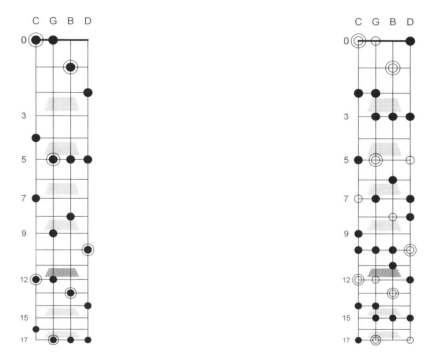

Figure 1: Left: positions the the notes in the C major chord. Right: positions of the notes in the C13sus4 chord.

How Do I Read These Charts?

On the **left hand side of the diagrams**, you will see numbers from 0 (the nut) to 17: these represent the number of semitones above the nut each horizontal line corresponds to. On a fretted instrument, the **horizontal lines** would correspond to frets, but if you have bought this book for use with an instrument without frets or fret markings, then you need to use your mind's eye to visualise these positions (doing so is an excellent mental exercise). The diagrams are scaled so that the location of the horizontal lines is in proportion to where they would appear on a real instrument, this will help you see visually and thus anticipate physically the contraction in finger spacing required in moving the scale further up the neck of the instrument. The large **solid dots** in the main diagrams show the locations of the notes of the chord in question. **Ringed dots** (around either a solid, or hollow dot) show the location of the root notes of the scale. **Hollow dots** are 'optional notes', see below for a further explanation.

With each fingerboard diagram are provided the notes in score notation and the defining degrees of the chord with respect to a major scale with the same root note (i.e. 'R' '2' '3' '4' '5' '6' '7'), together with their modifications (i.e. ♭ or ♯). For example, a C major chord[1] would be denoted R 3 5 and the C minor chord as R ♭3 5. The letter 'R' stands for root, '3' (=E for the C major) is the third tone in a major scale (the Ionian mode) starting on the root note (=C in this case) and '5' (=G here) is the 5th tone. Those familiar with chordal theory will know that is is the '3' versus '♭3' that give the major and minor chords their distinctive happy and sad sounds respectively.

How do I Choose Which Notes to Play?

It depends what you are trying to achieve. If you are playing arpeggios, then you would normally play all notes in the chord in succession. If you are using the banjo to accompany other musicians, then other parts of the chord may be contributed by other instruments, so you don't necessarily need to play those tones. It is not necessarily the case that you will have enough fingers (or conveniently tuned strings) to be able to play all notes of a full chord in any case, particularly the more complex jazz chords.

If your chord sheet indicates a C major for the next bar, then you could look at the diagram for the C major chord and pick out ANY reachable set of notes: playing these notes will sound 'good' over the C major chord (success). Even if you do not include all the different tones indicated in the chord, it will still sound good, but then you have likely played a chord of a different name; in my opinion, this does not matter. Sometimes you do not have enough spare fingers and/or strings to execute a particular chord e.g. the six notes of the C13sus4 chord. In this book, I have adopted the following convention: that 9ths (9 ♭9 or ♯9) can replace the root, and that the 5th can be replaced by a ♭5 (=♯ 11), a ♯5, or a 13th. In the diagrams, I have indicated optional notes as hollow dots, a **ringed hollow dot** is an optional note that also happens to be a root note.

If you have played all the notes of the chord, but out of order, then you may have played an inversion of some kind. For example, a major chord (R 3 5) can be played as 3 5 R (1st inversion) or 5 R 3 (2nd inversion). If the lowest note is not the root and your chosen fingering gives emphasis to it, then you have what is known as a slash chord. The lowest note need not necessarily be a part of the chord.

The slash chord C/E is obtained by playing the notes of a C major chord, but giving emphasis to an E in the bass. In fact often the note on the right of the slash is delivered *by* the bass, but I'm sure there will be plenty of occasions when you may wish to deliver that note yourself. The notes of C/E are therefore E (lowest tone, and with emphasis) and C, E and G (or a convenient inversion). I have chosen not to include slash chords explicitly in this book, though you could construct one by adding a bass note of the appropriate type. Slash chords give the feeling of a need for resolution and can be used to great effect.

Author's Notes on this Edition

To avoid over-cluttering the diagrams, I have not included the names of the notes (or scale degrees) on the fingerboard diagrams. I have, however, included for each scale the notes in score notation. In all cases, I have elected to use sharps to indicate accidentals. The reason for this is that these scales could appear in any key and technically, the precise choice of accidentals as a combination of sharps and/or flats would be determined by the key of the piece at the point the notes appeared in the music. To present all possible enharmonic equivalents would not be an efficient use of space.

In the score, I have not made a distinction between 9ths and 2nds, nor between 11ths and 4ths nor 13ths and 6ths. Thus for example, I have notated in score the Cadd9 chord, defined by the scale degrees R 3 5 9 (or C E G D in notes), as R 2 3 5 (C D E G, in notes).

I welcome **constructive** feedback on my book. Please feel free to contact me with comments by email using the address `benjamin.cello.mad.taylor@googlemail.com`. In particular, if you would like a scales or arpeggios book for a stringed instrument in an unusual tuning, please don't hesitate to let me know.

---

[1]or indeed any other major chord

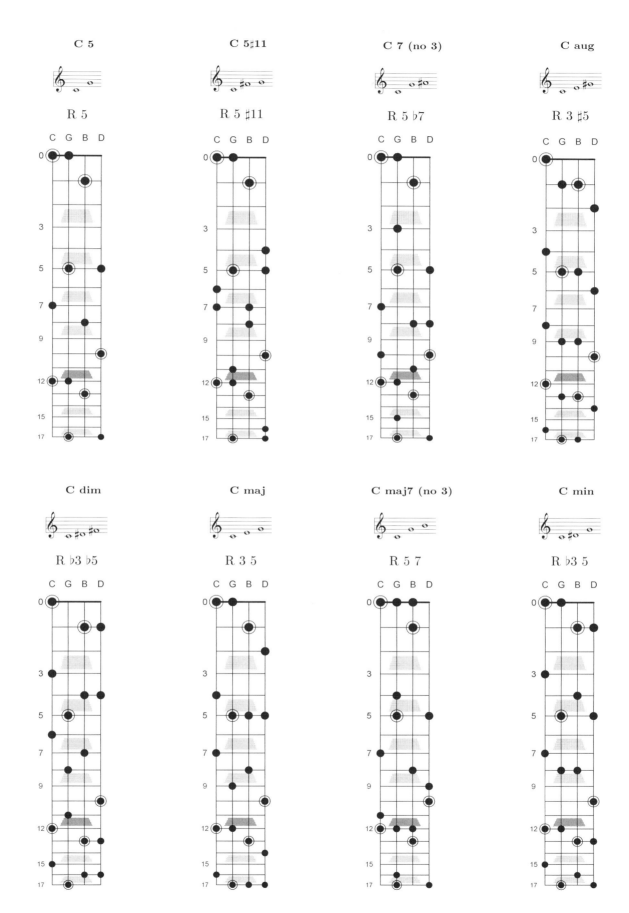

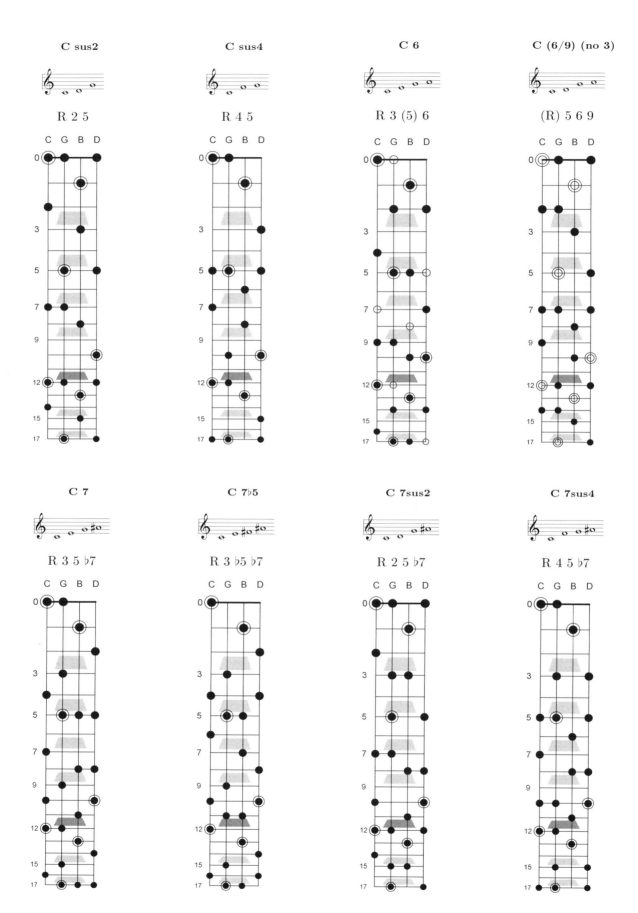

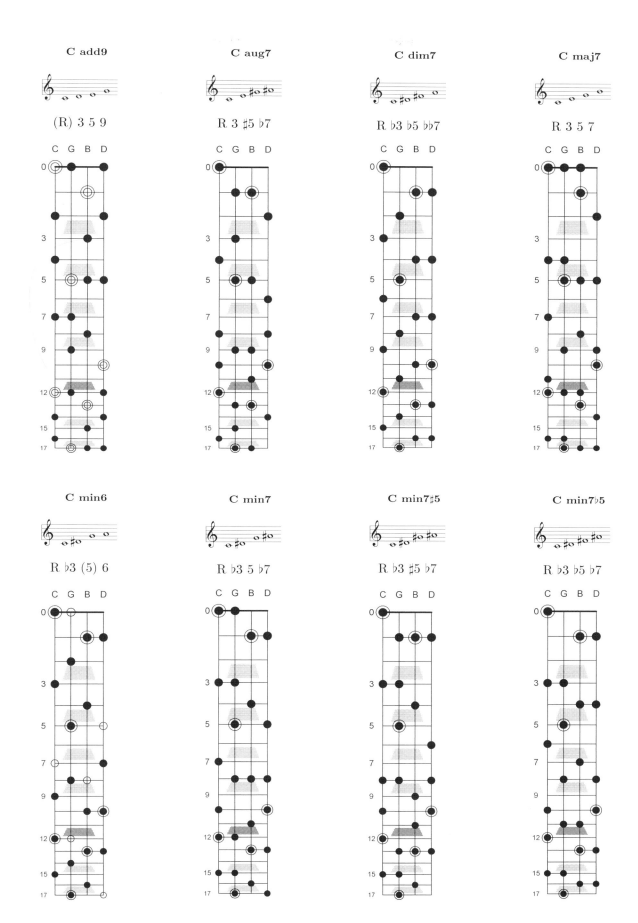

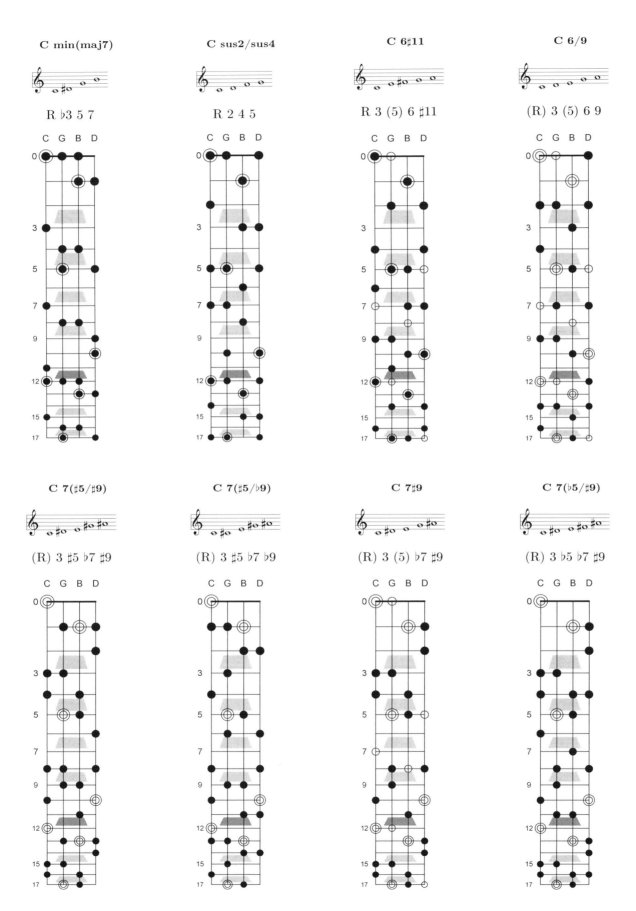

18

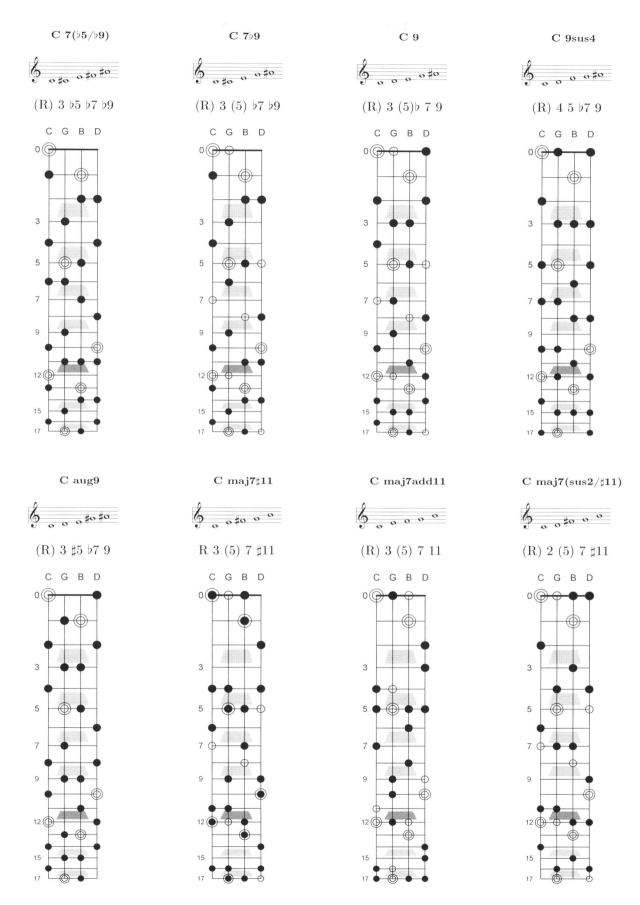

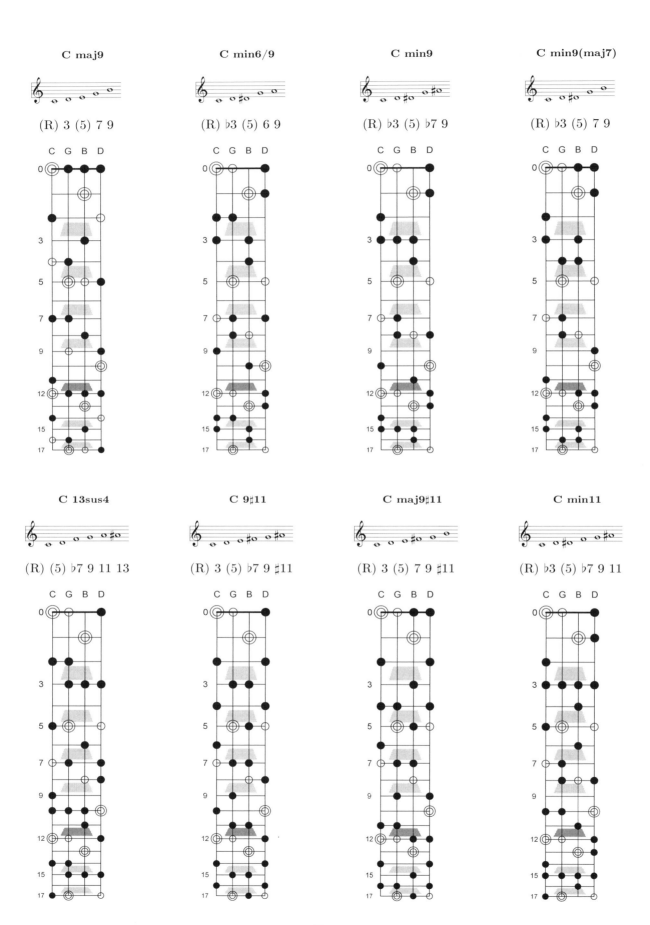

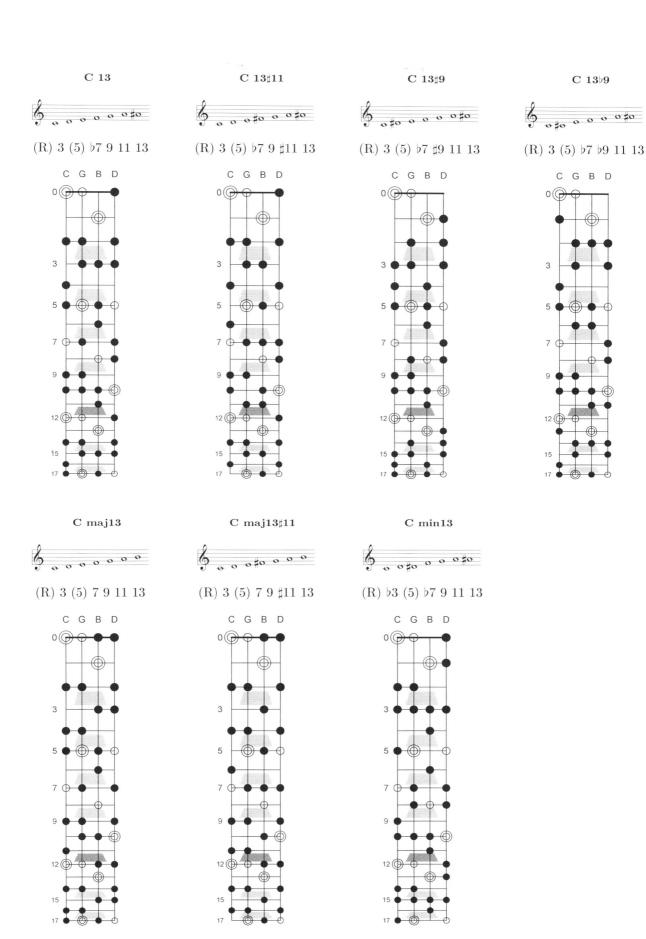

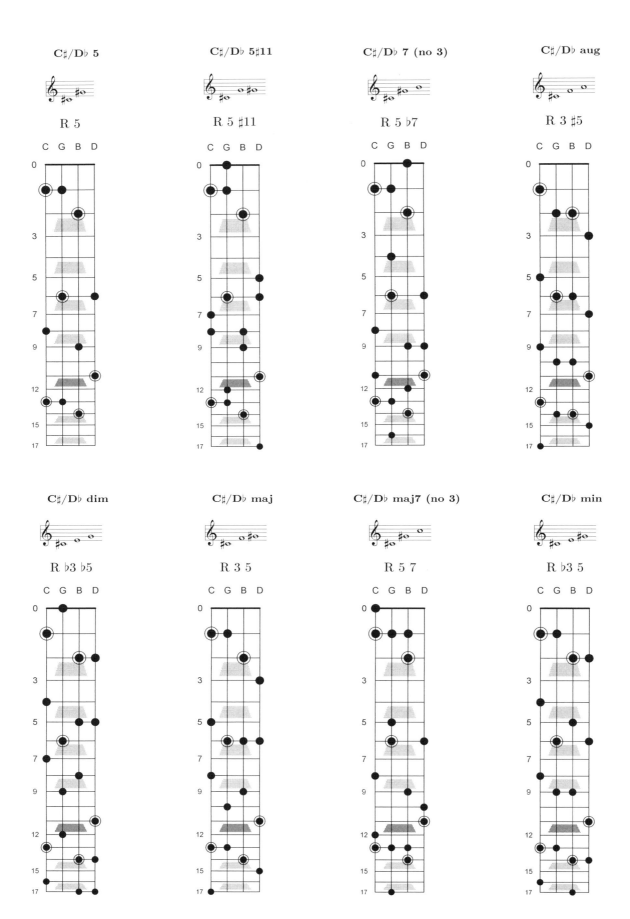

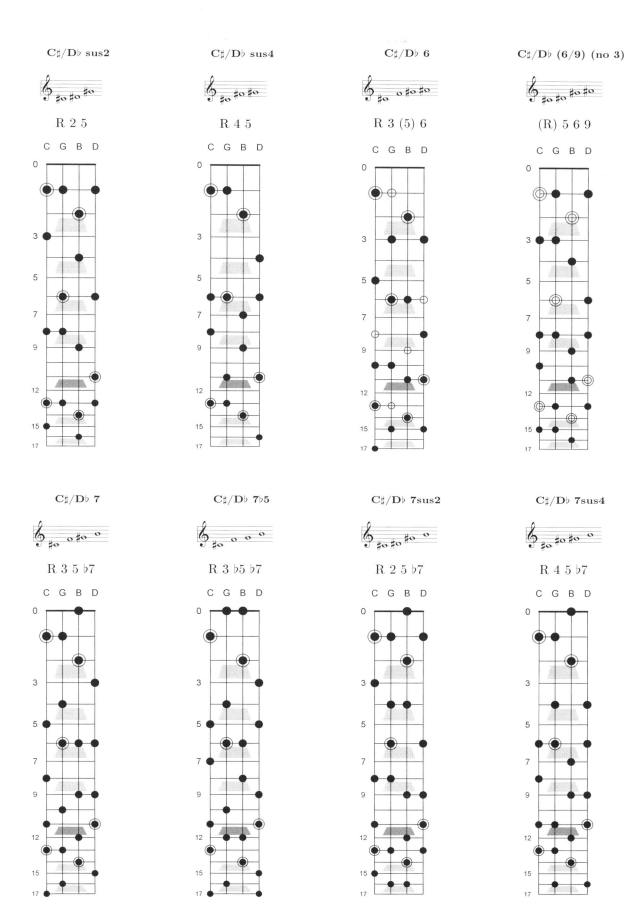

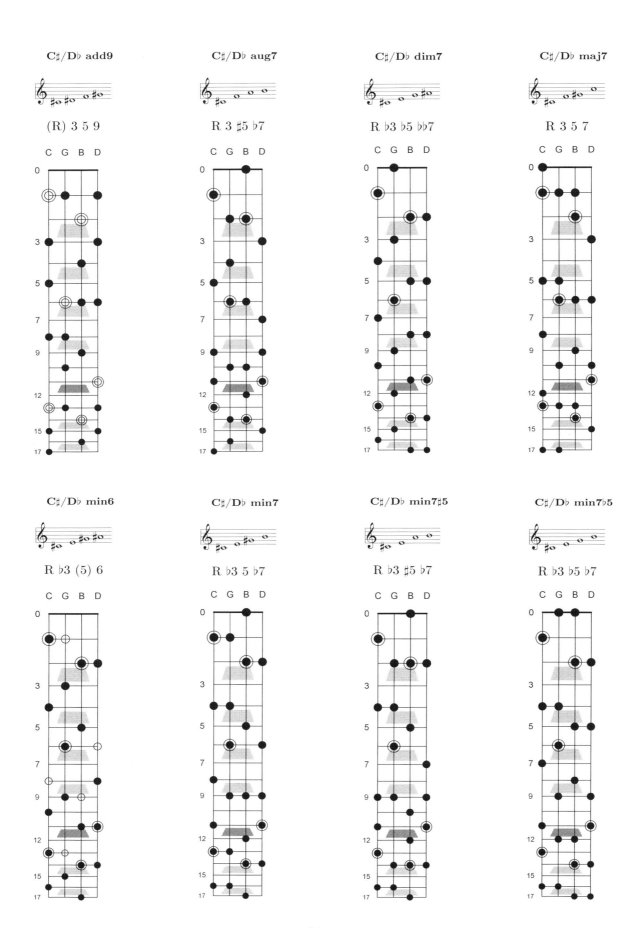

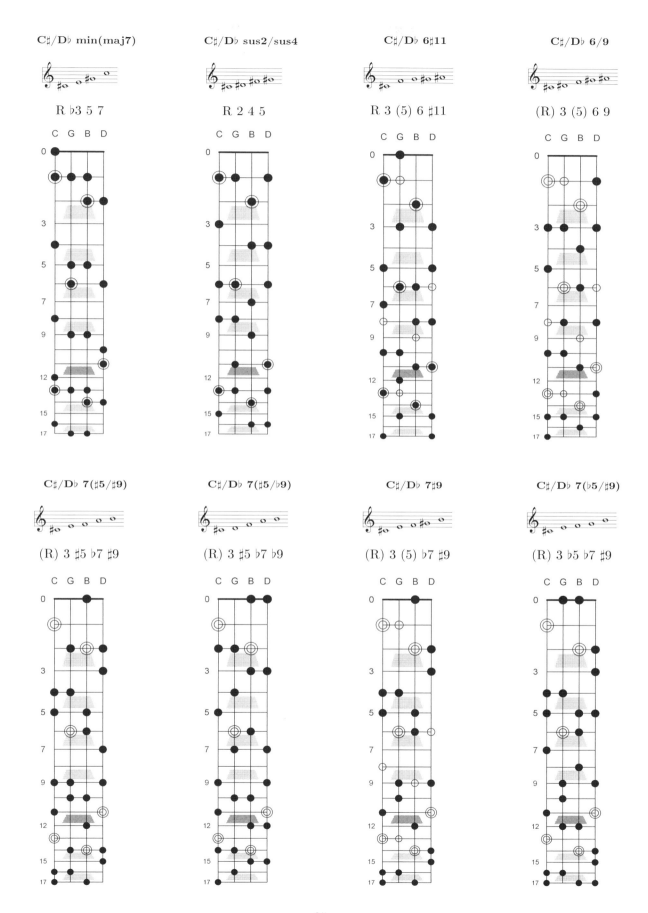

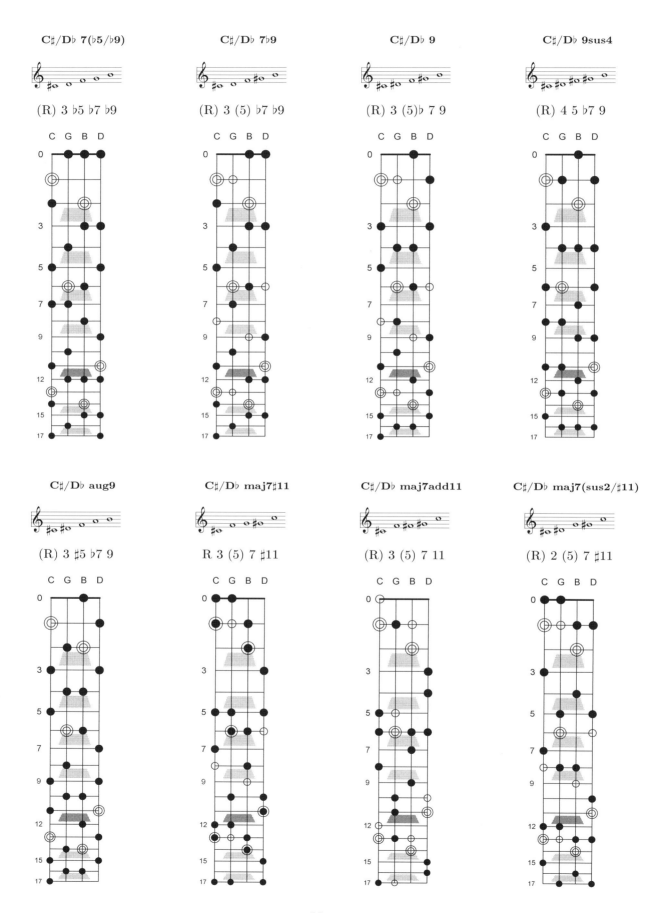

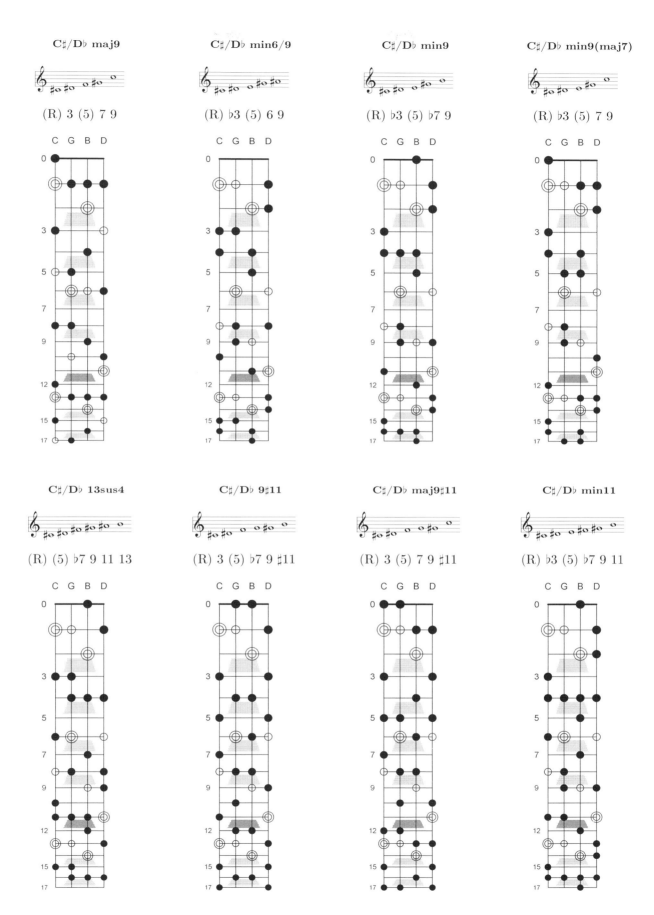

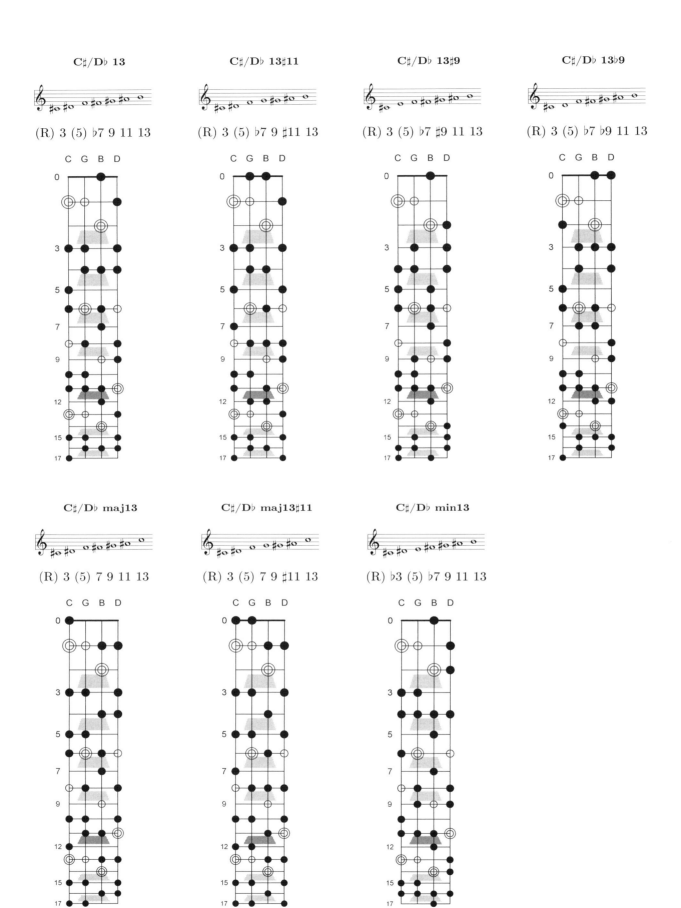

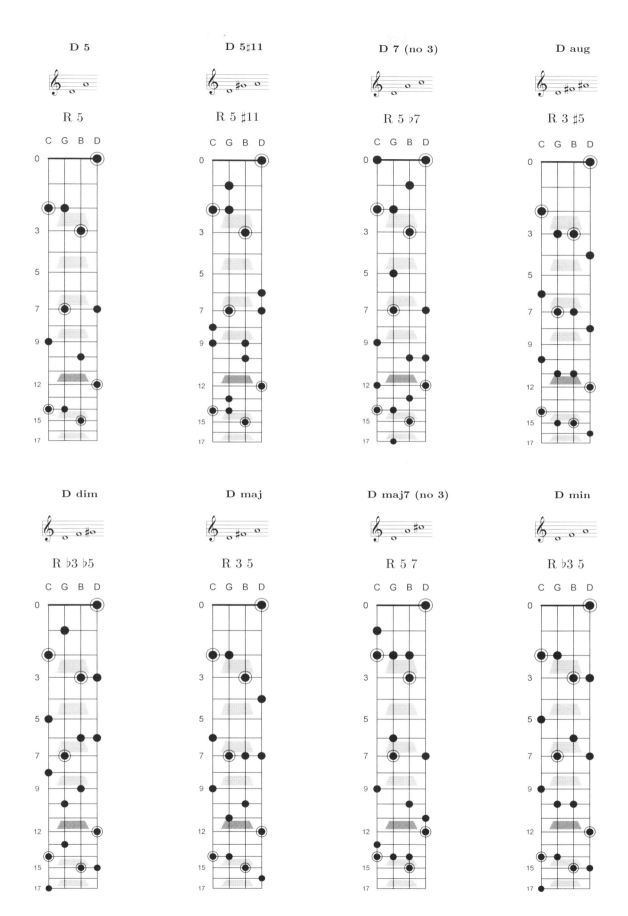

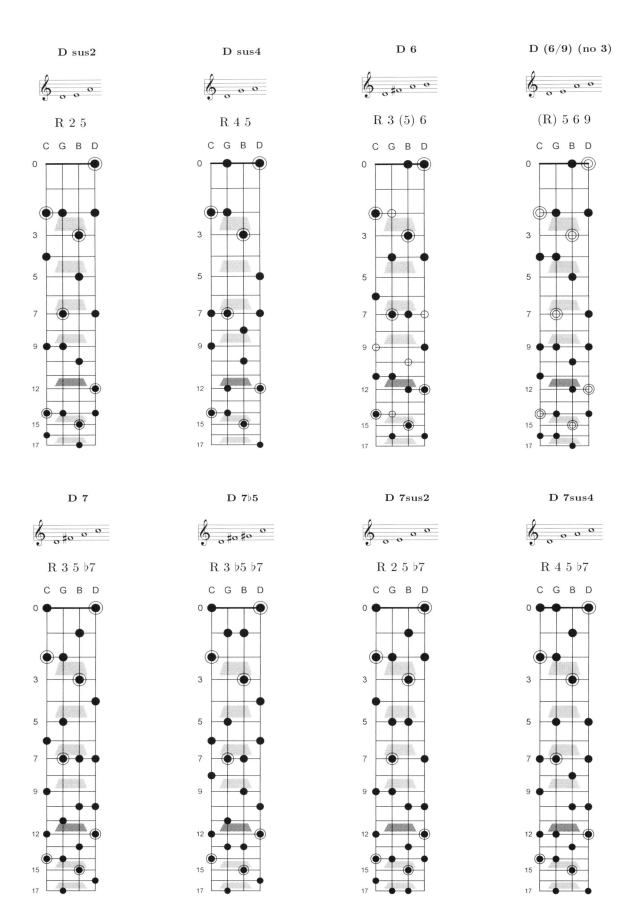

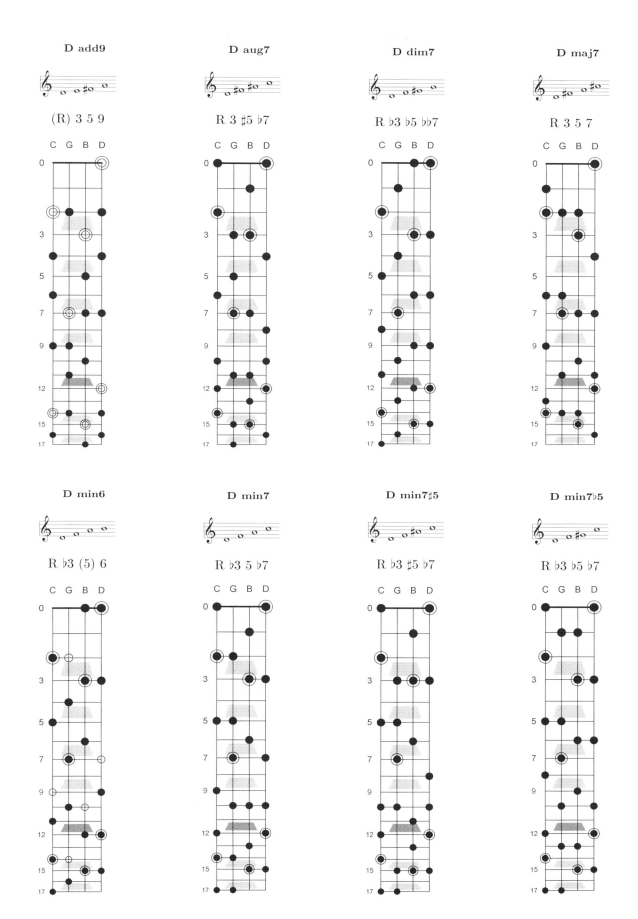

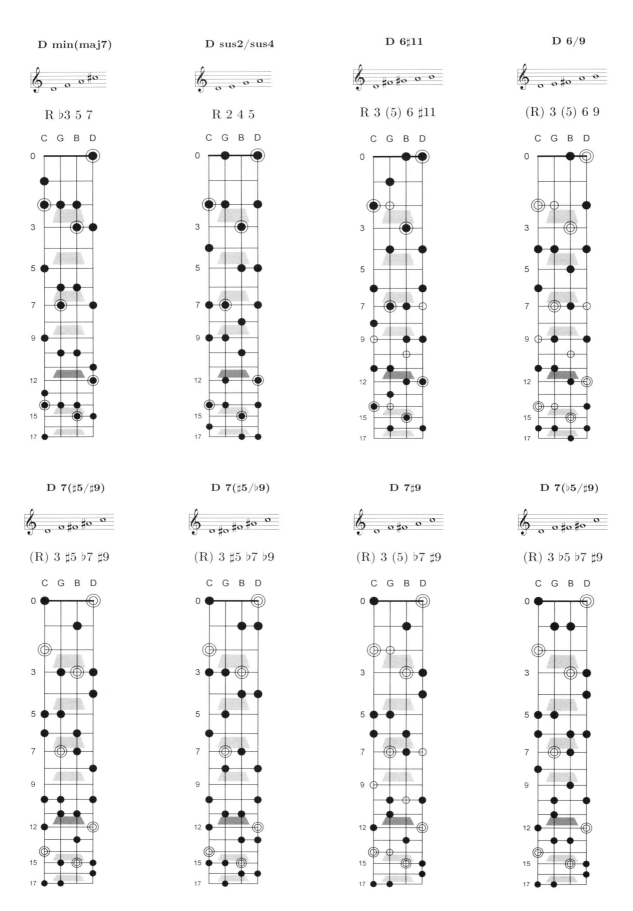

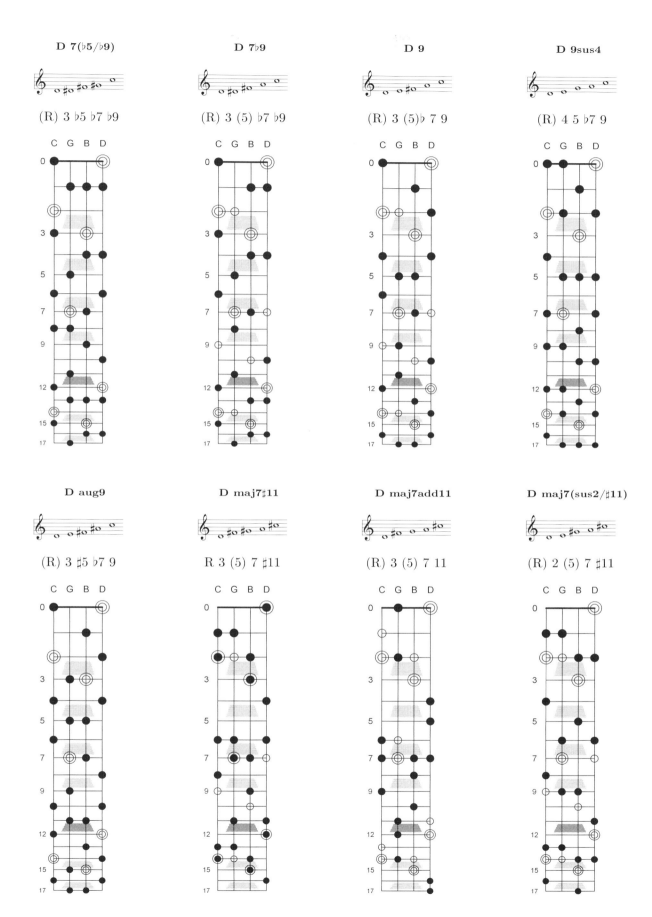

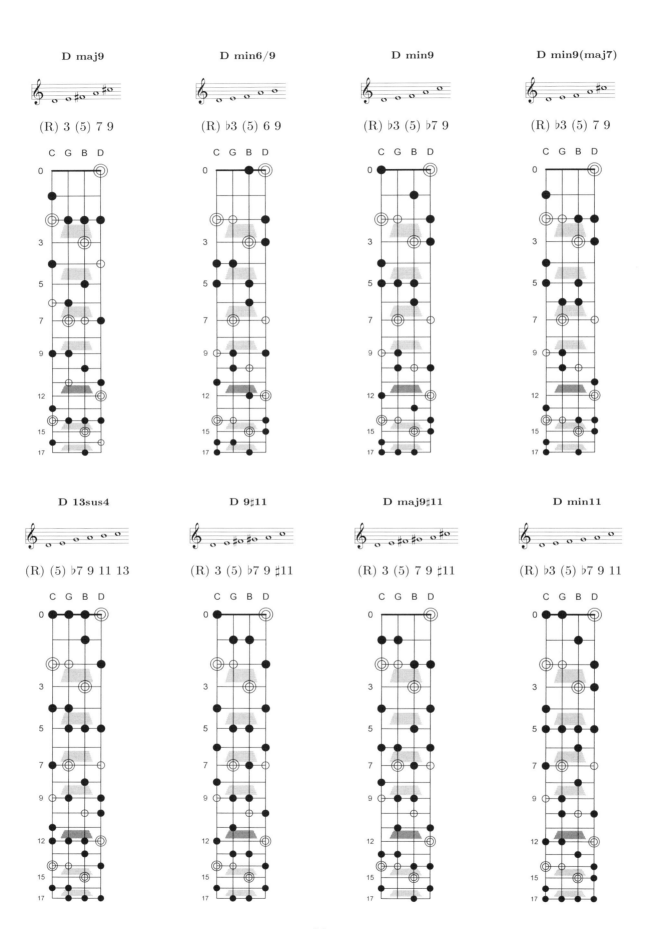

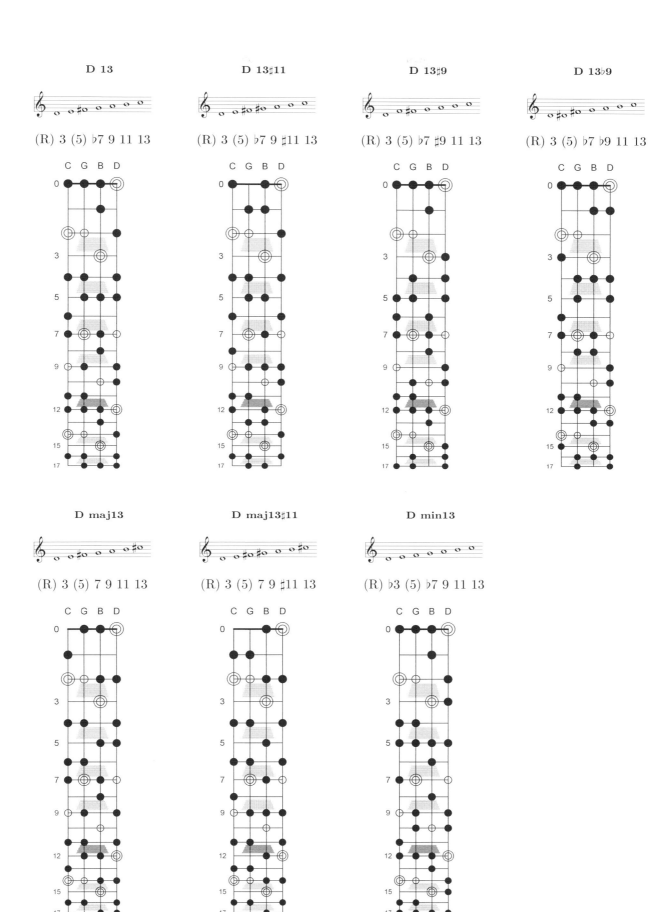

D 13

(R) 3 (5) ♭7 9 11 13

D 13♯11

(R) 3 (5) ♭7 9 ♯11 13

D 13♯9

(R) 3 (5) ♭7 ♯9 11 13

D 13♭9

(R) 3 (5) ♭7 ♭9 11 13

D maj13

(R) 3 (5) 7 9 11 13

D maj13♯11

(R) 3 (5) 7 9 ♯11 13

D min13

(R) ♭3 (5) ♭7 9 11 13

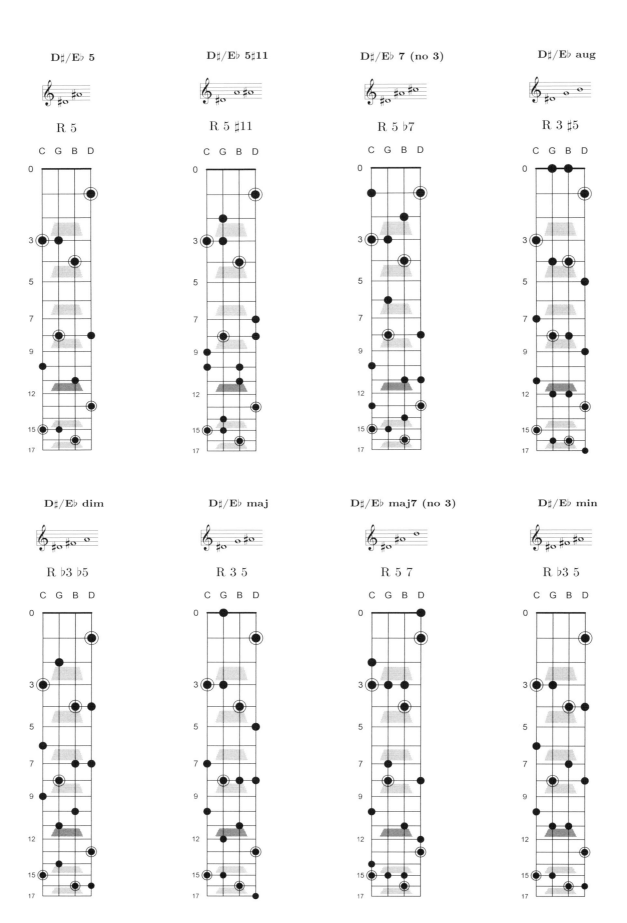

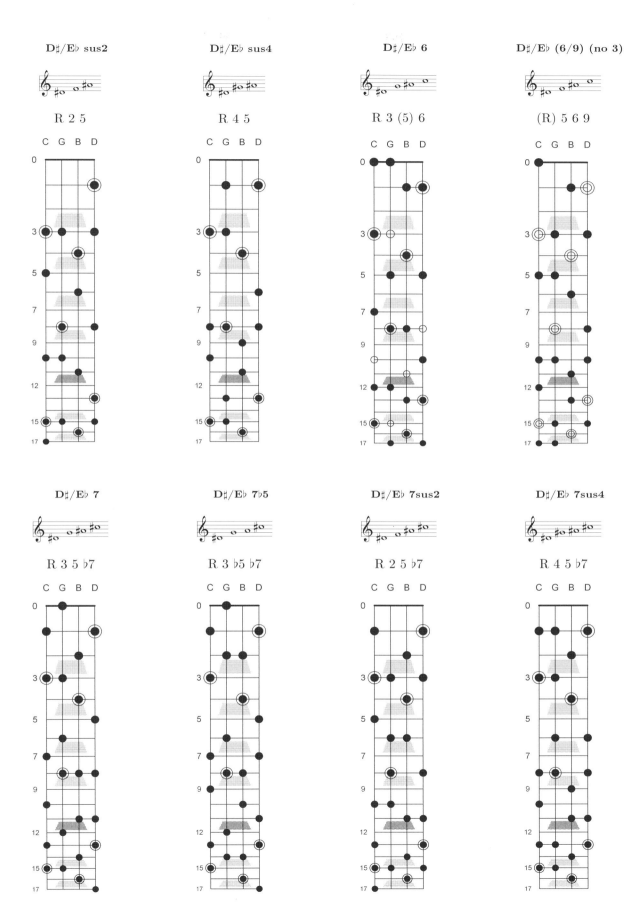

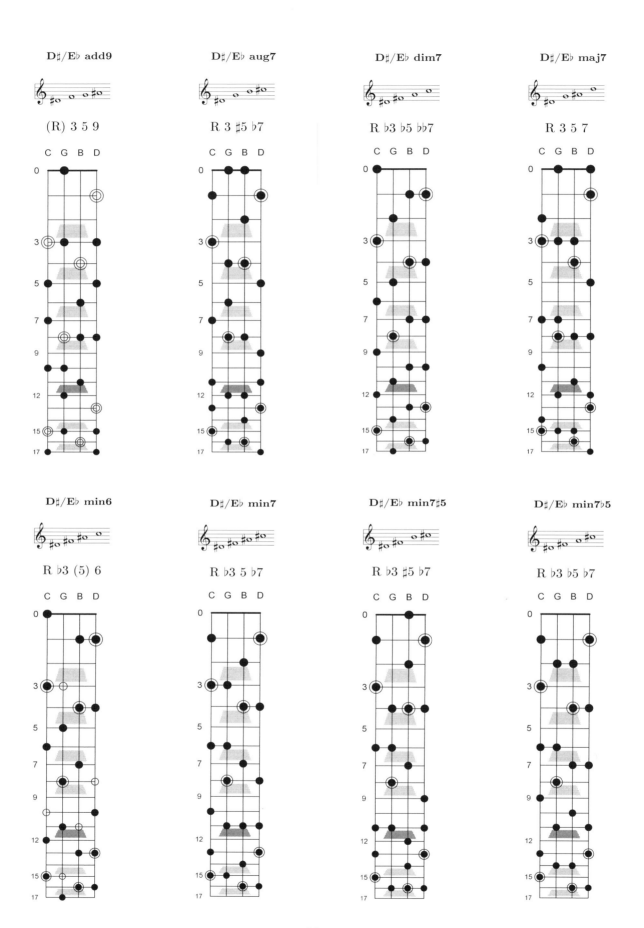

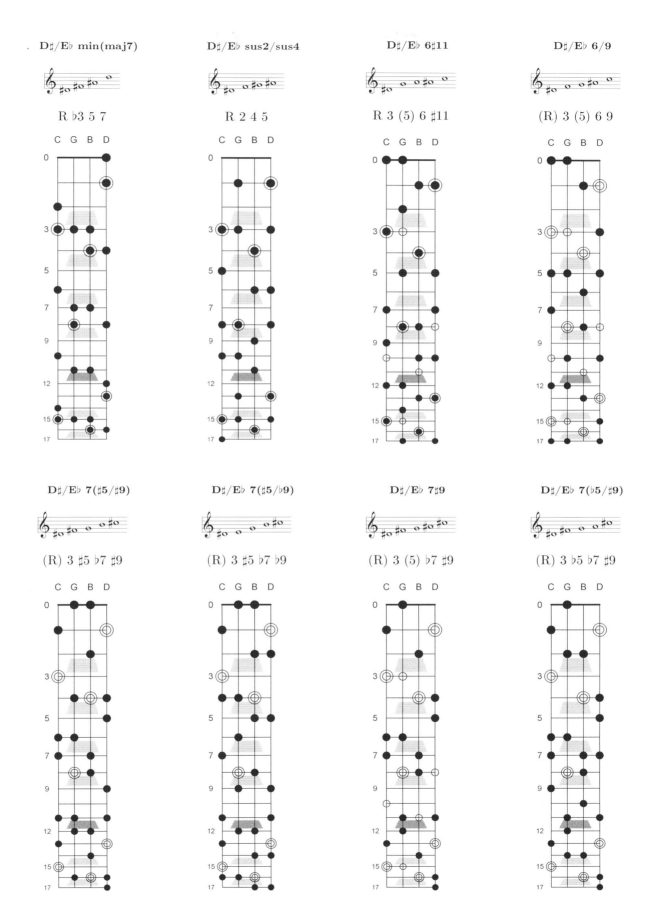

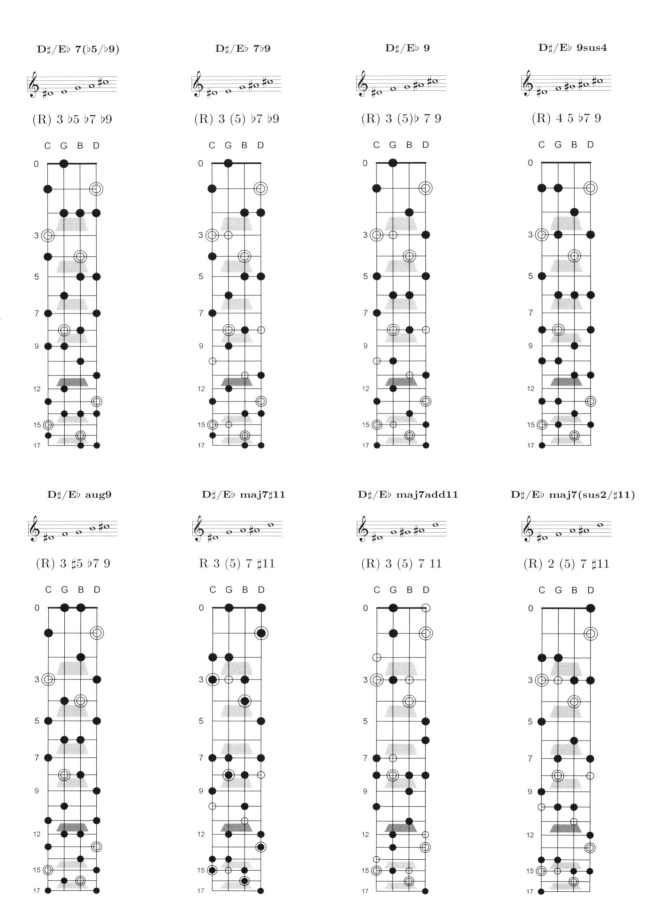

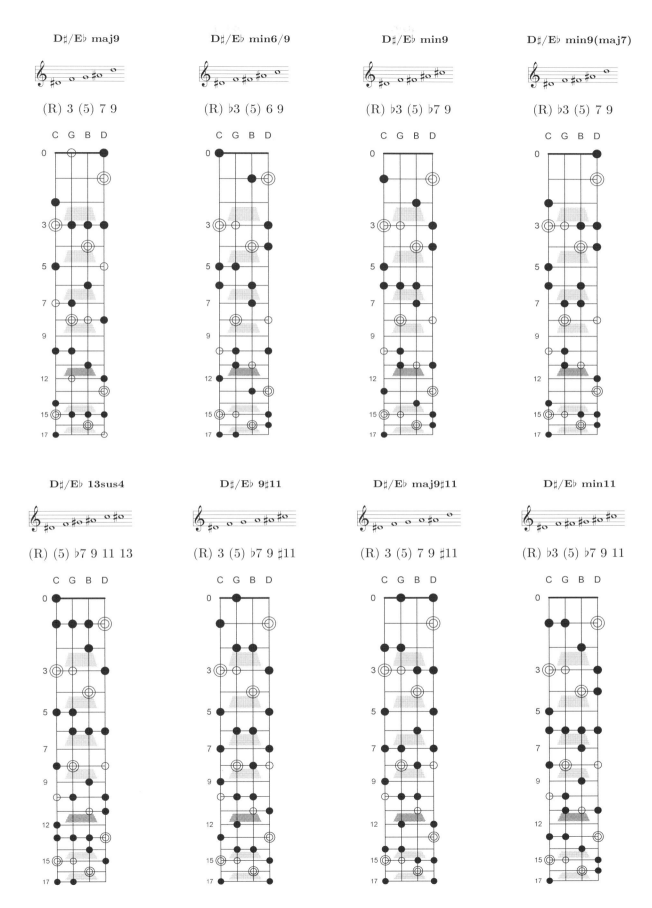

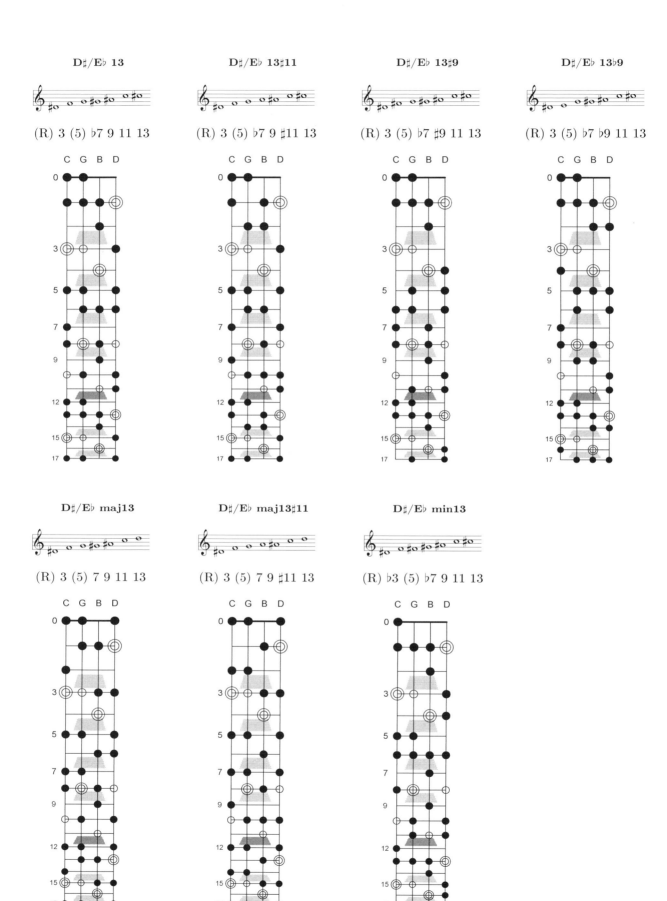

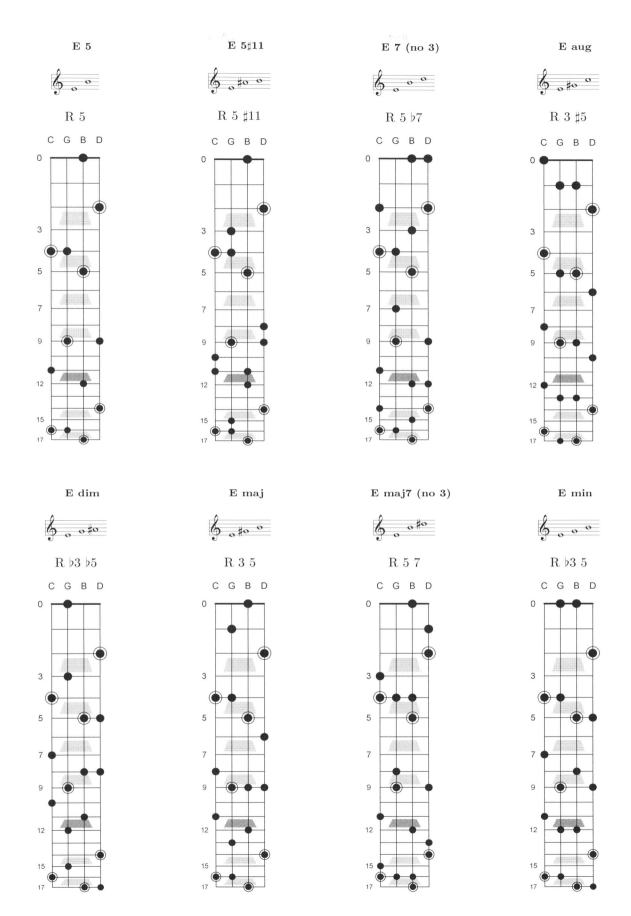

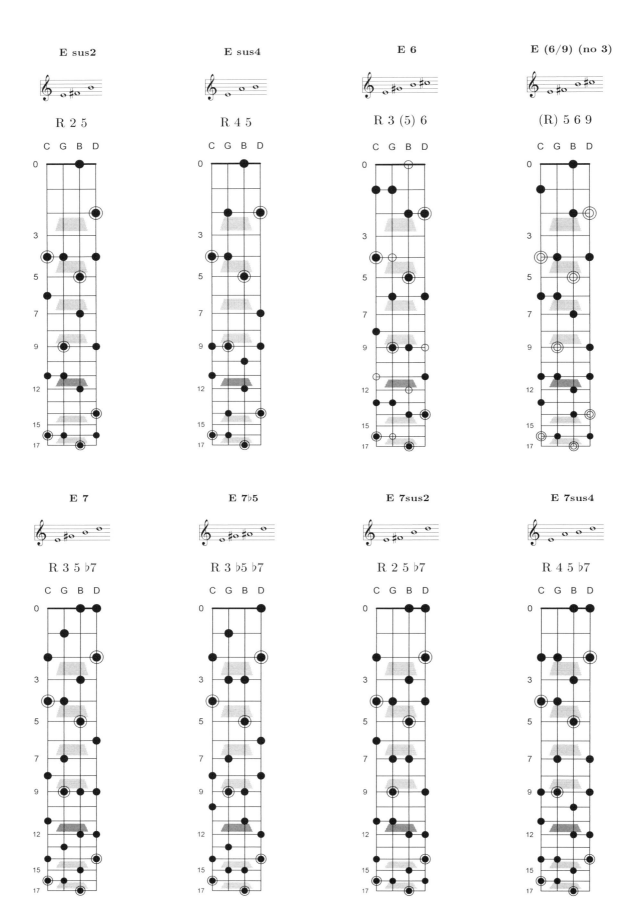

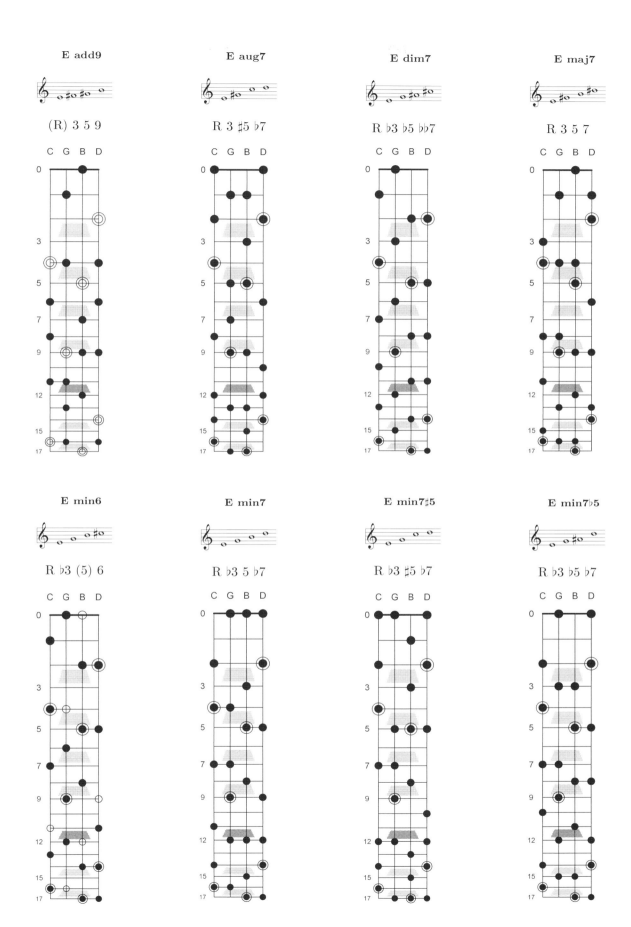

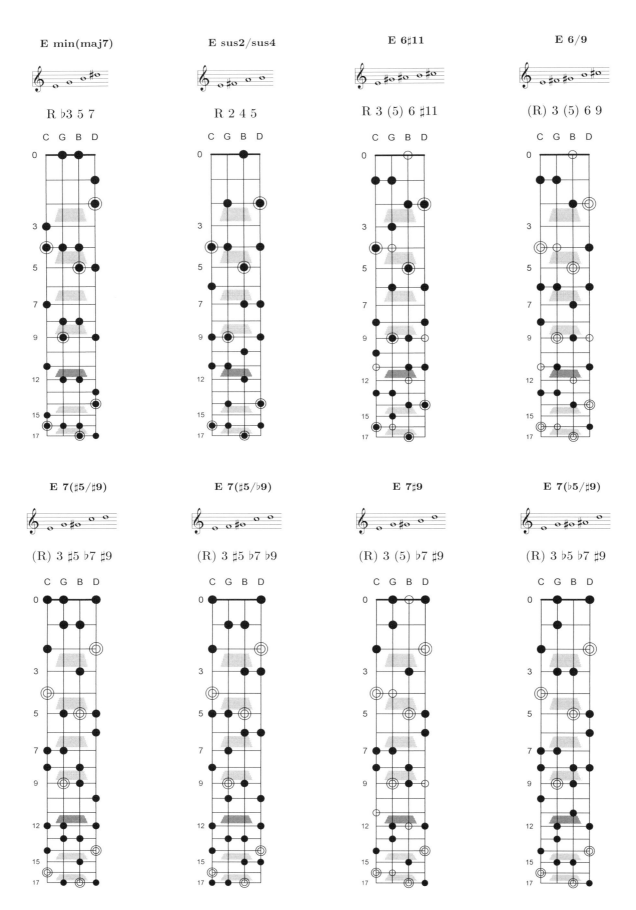

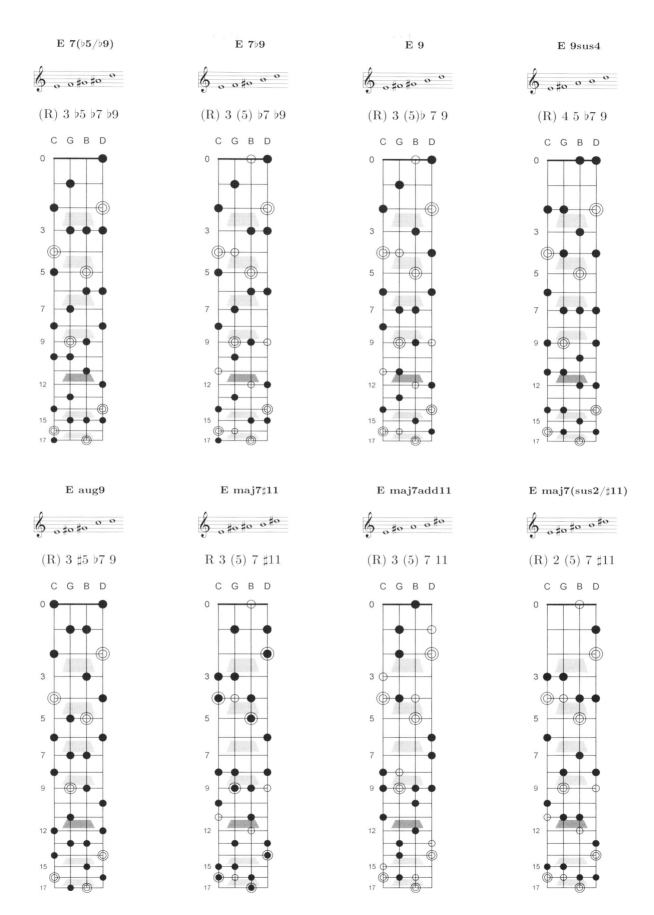

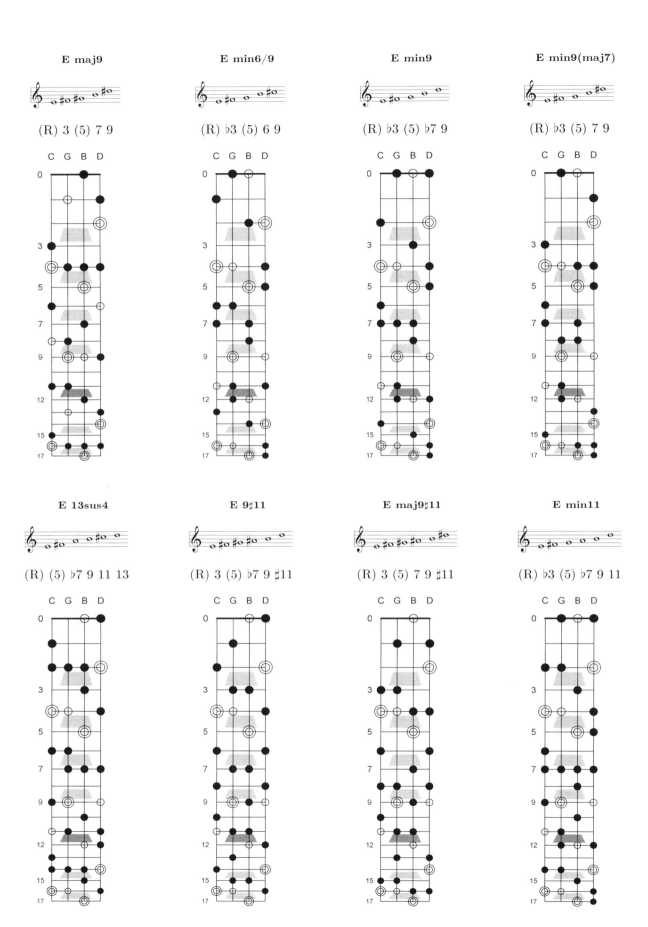

48

E 13

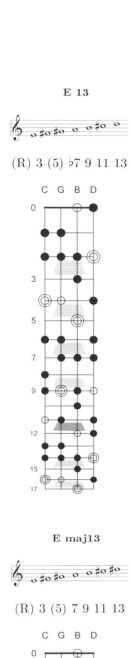

(R) 3 (5) ♭7 9 11 13

E 13♯11

(R) 3 (5) ♭7 9 ♯11 13

E 13♯9

(R) 3 (5) ♭7 ♯9 11 13

E 13♭9

(R) 3 (5) ♭7 ♭9 11 13

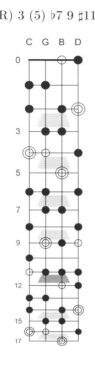
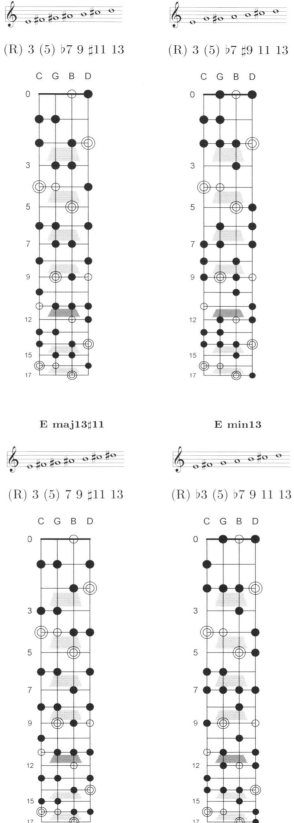
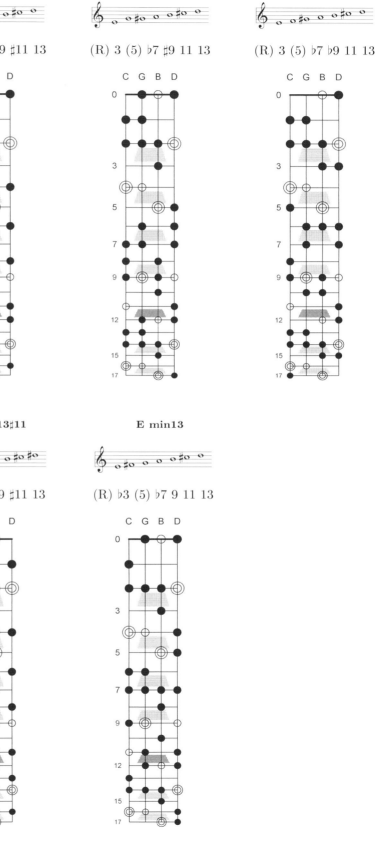

E maj13

(R) 3 (5) 7 9 11 13

E maj13♯11

(R) 3 (5) 7 9 ♯11 13

E min13

(R) ♭3 (5) ♭7 9 11 13

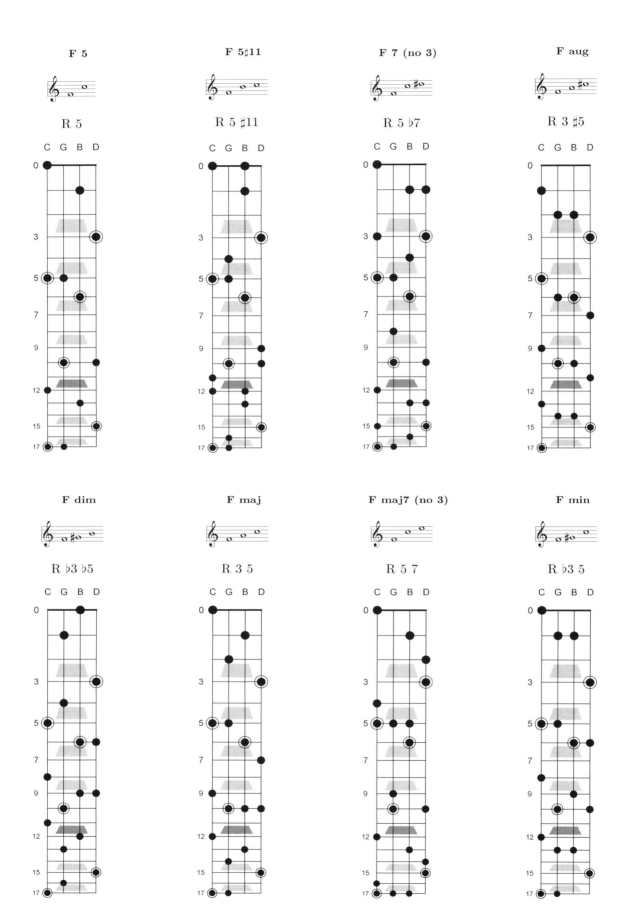

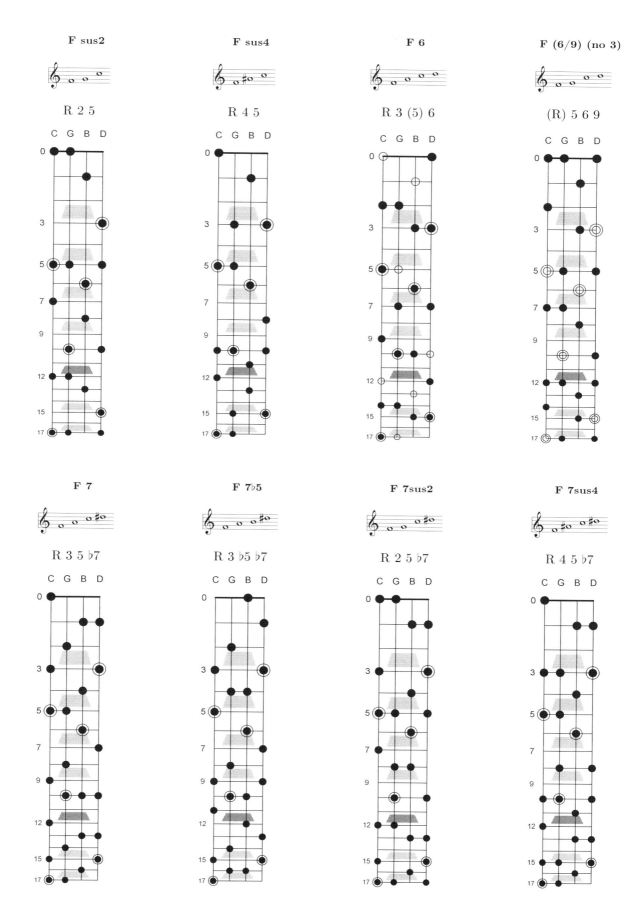

51

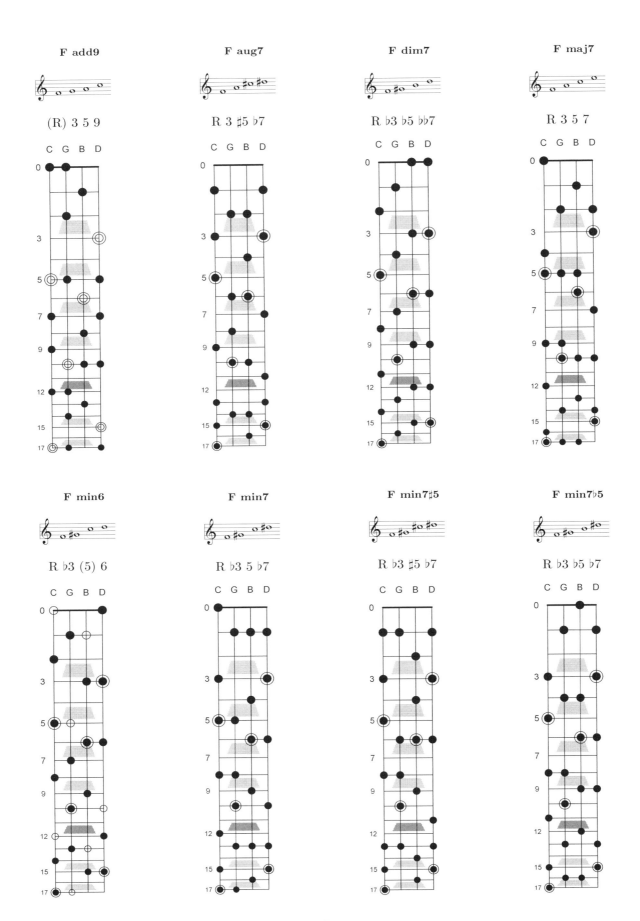

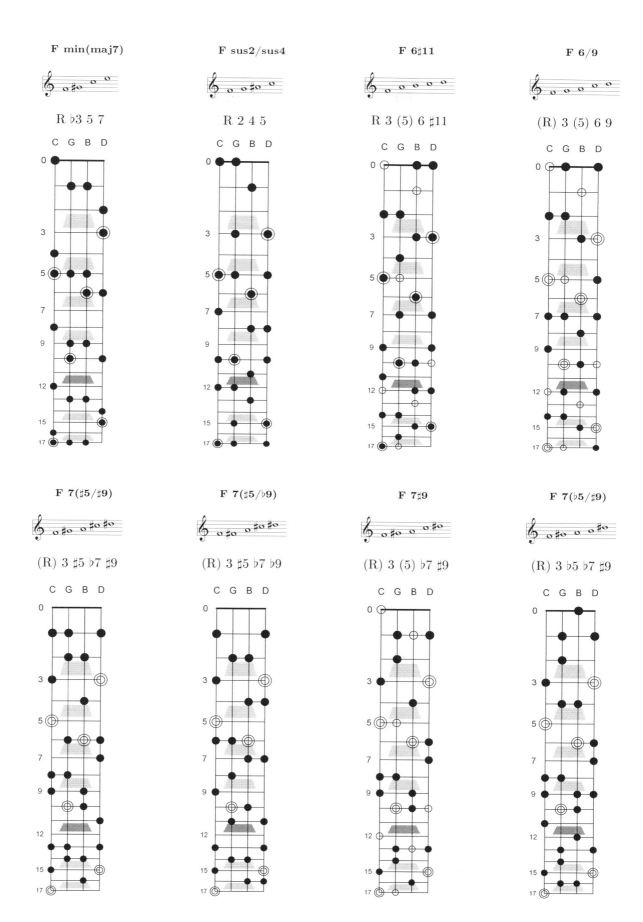

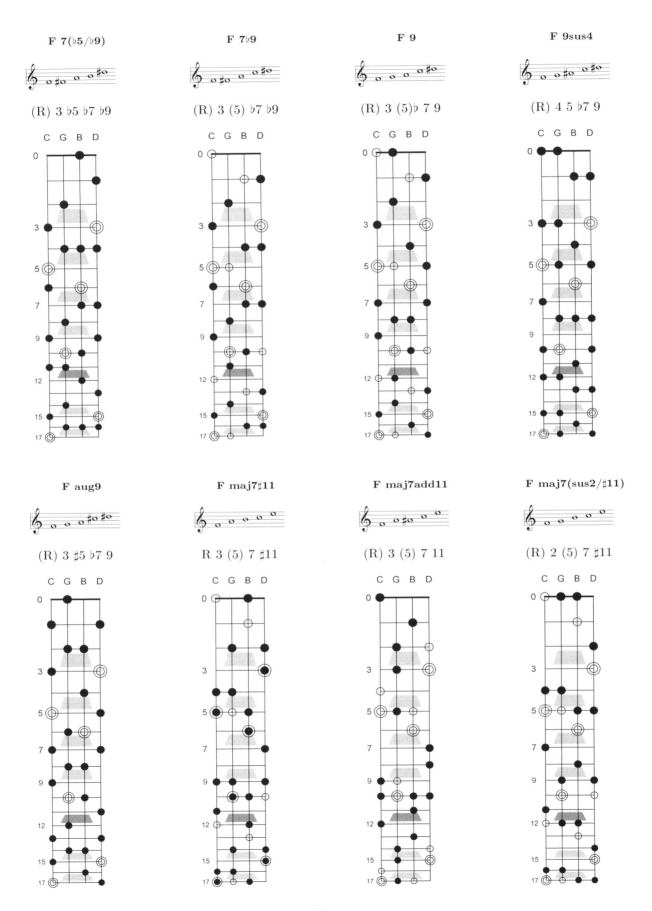

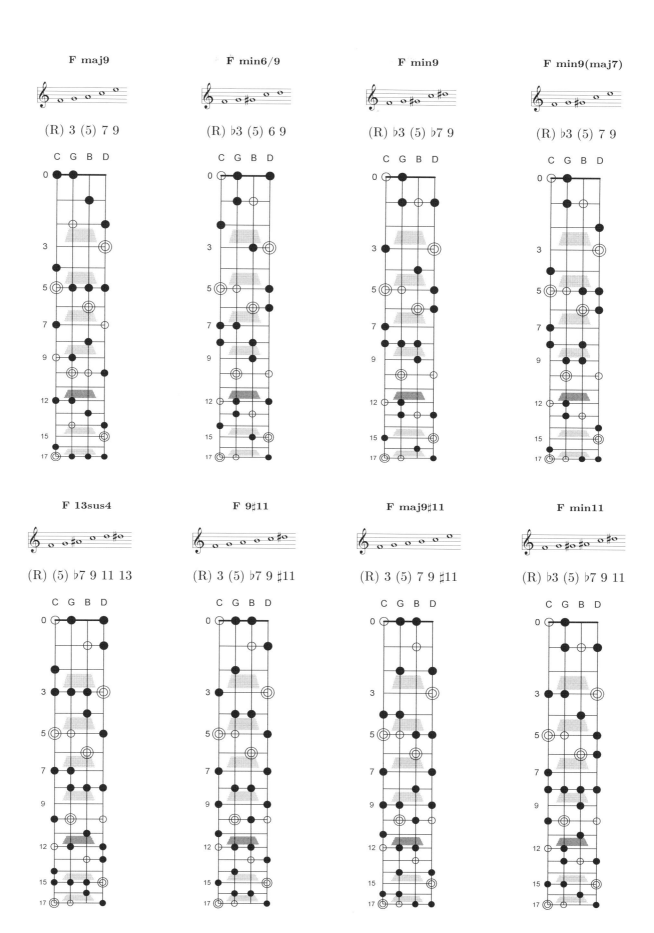

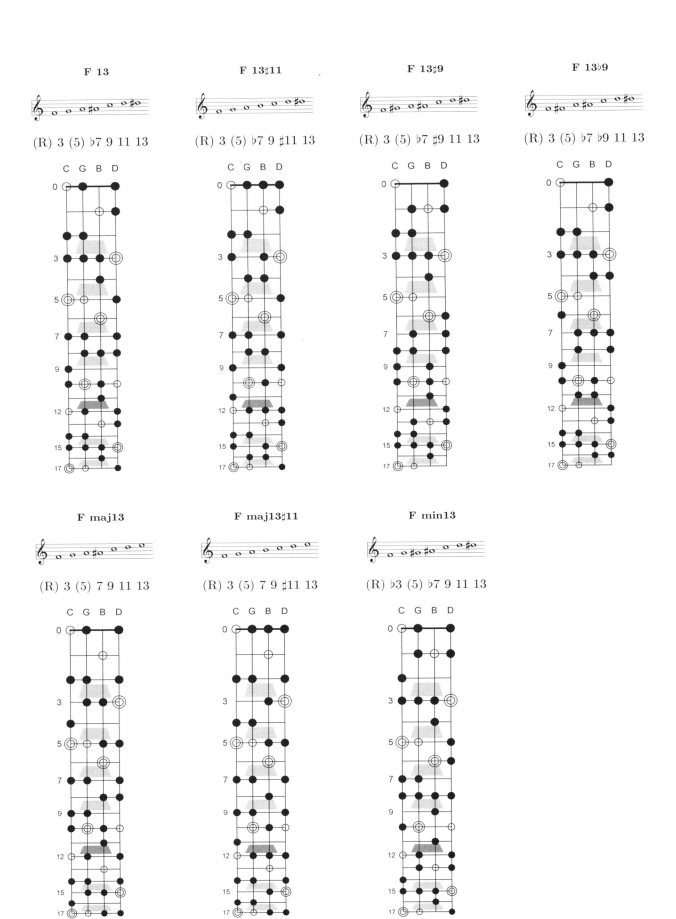

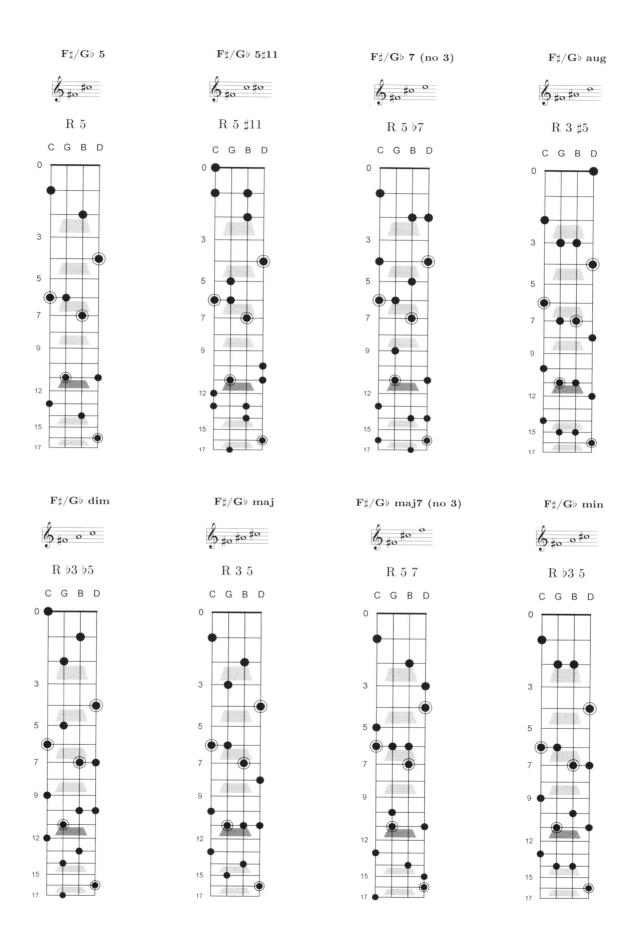

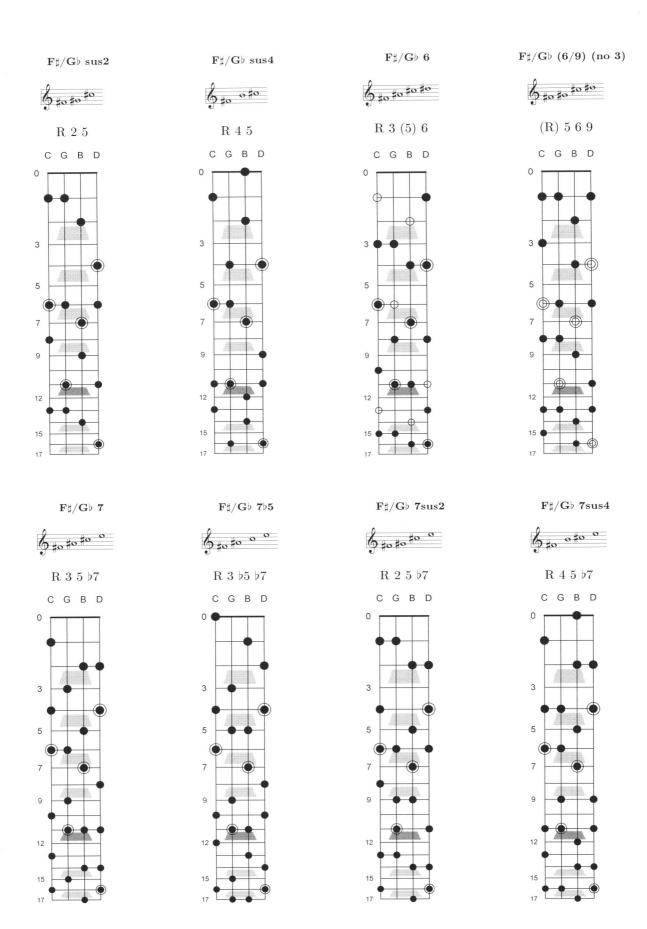

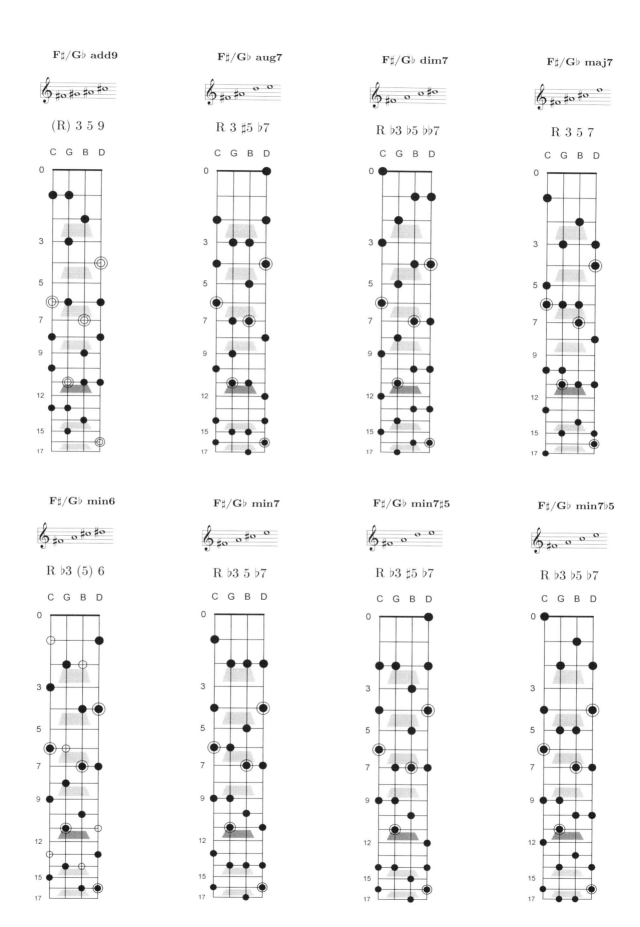

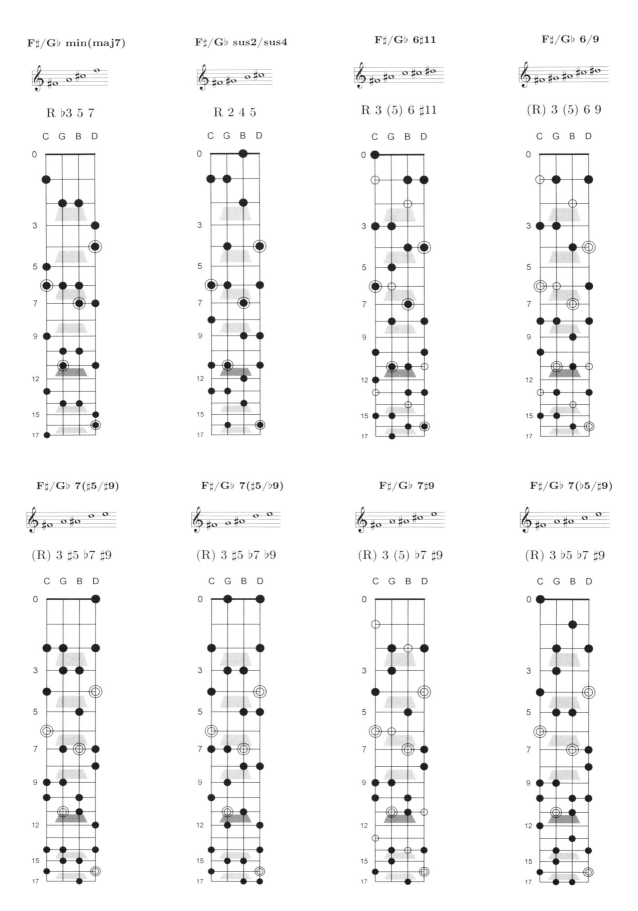

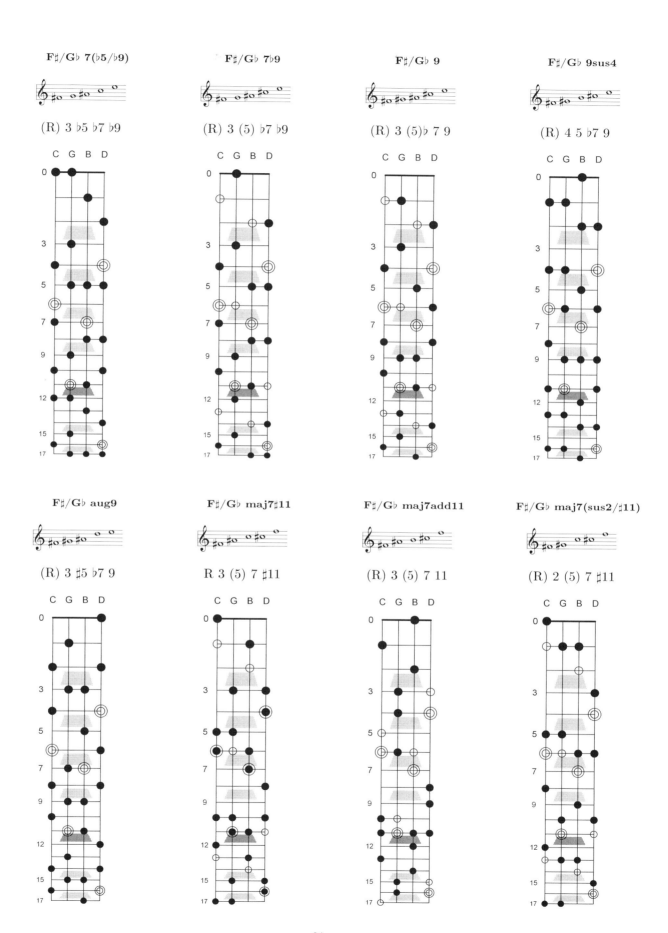

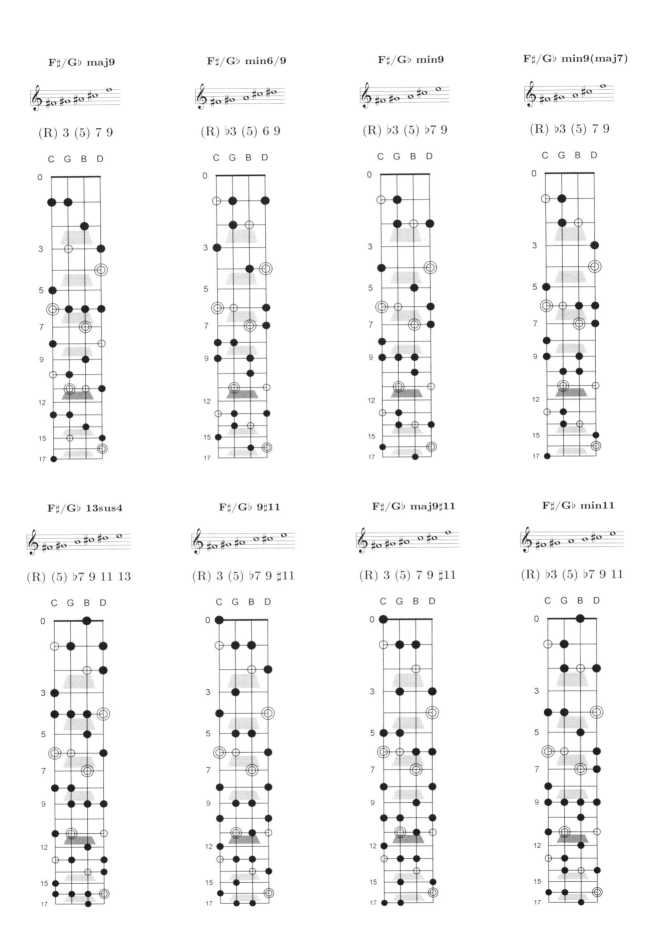

F♯/G♭ maj9

(R) 3 (5) 7 9

F♯/G♭ min6/9

(R) ♭3 (5) 6 9

F♯/G♭ min9

(R) ♭3 (5) ♭7 9

F♯/G♭ min9(maj7)

(R) ♭3 (5) 7 9

F♯/G♭ 13sus4

(R) (5) ♭7 9 11 13

F♯/G♭ 9♯11

(R) 3 (5) ♭7 9 ♯11

F♯/G♭ maj9♯11

(R) 3 (5) 7 9 ♯11

F♯/G♭ min11

(R) ♭3 (5) ♭7 9 11

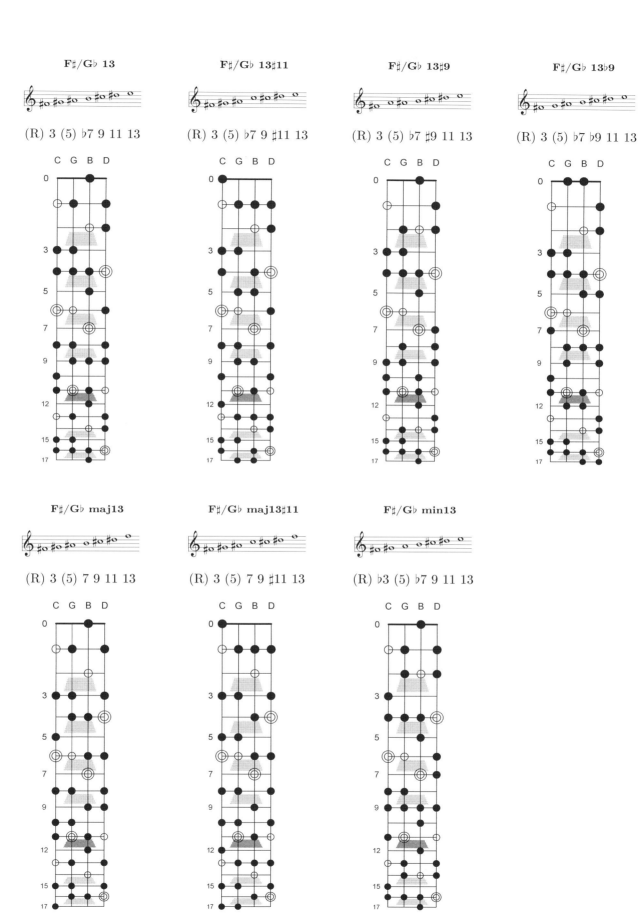

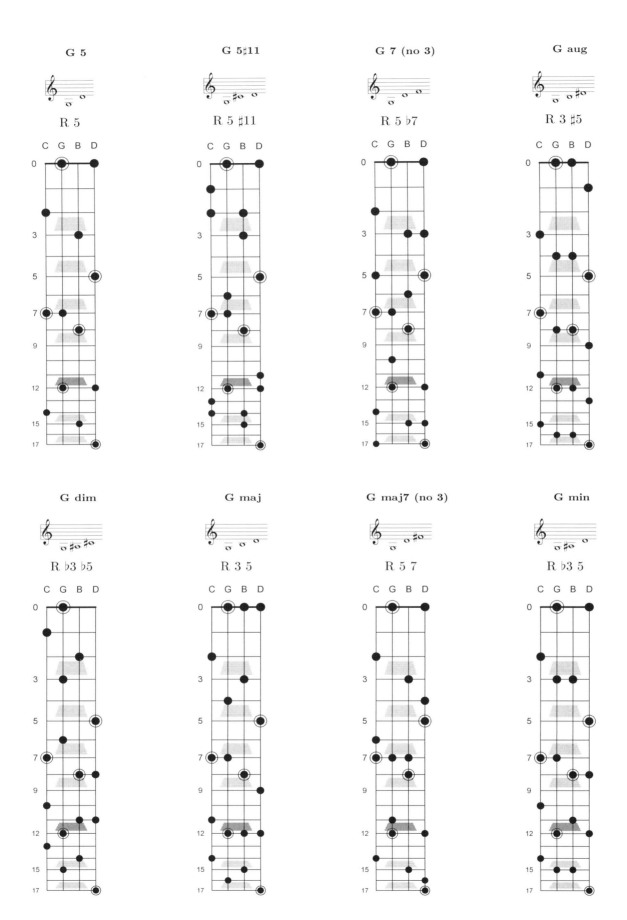

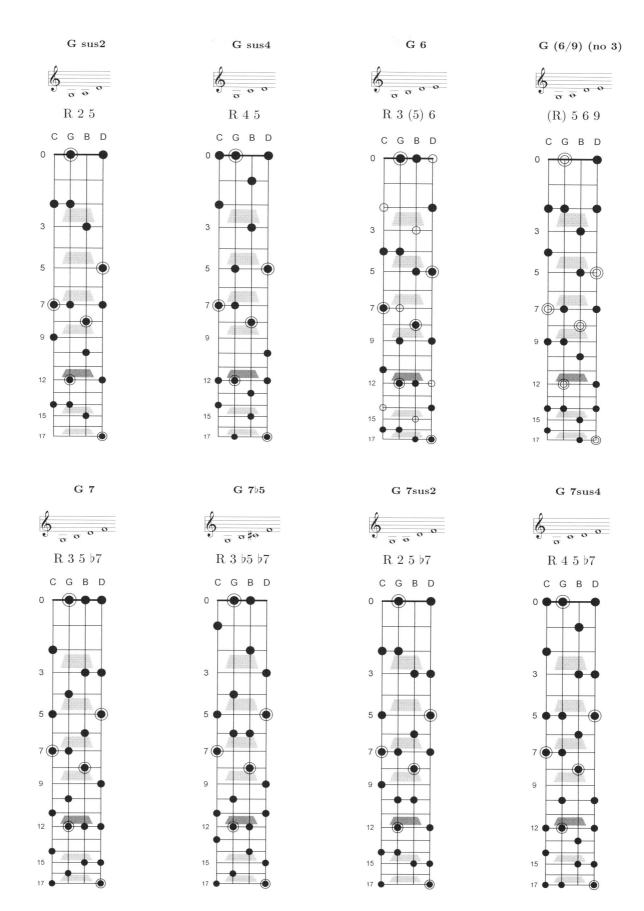

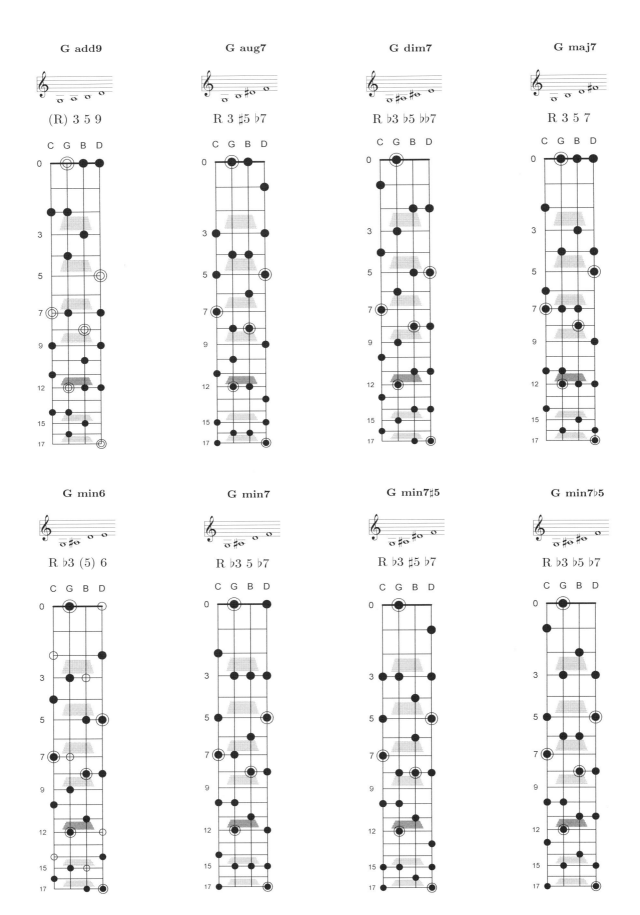

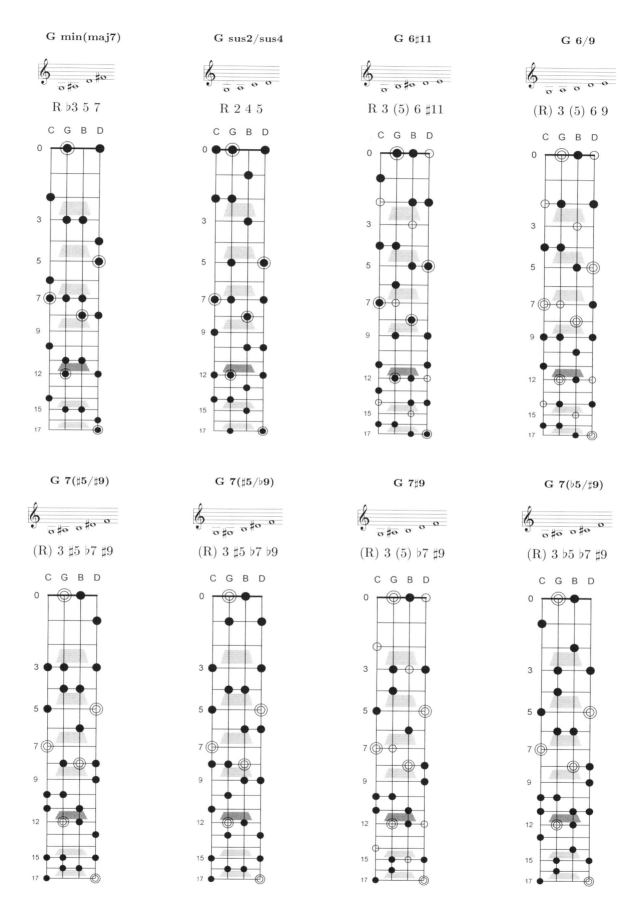

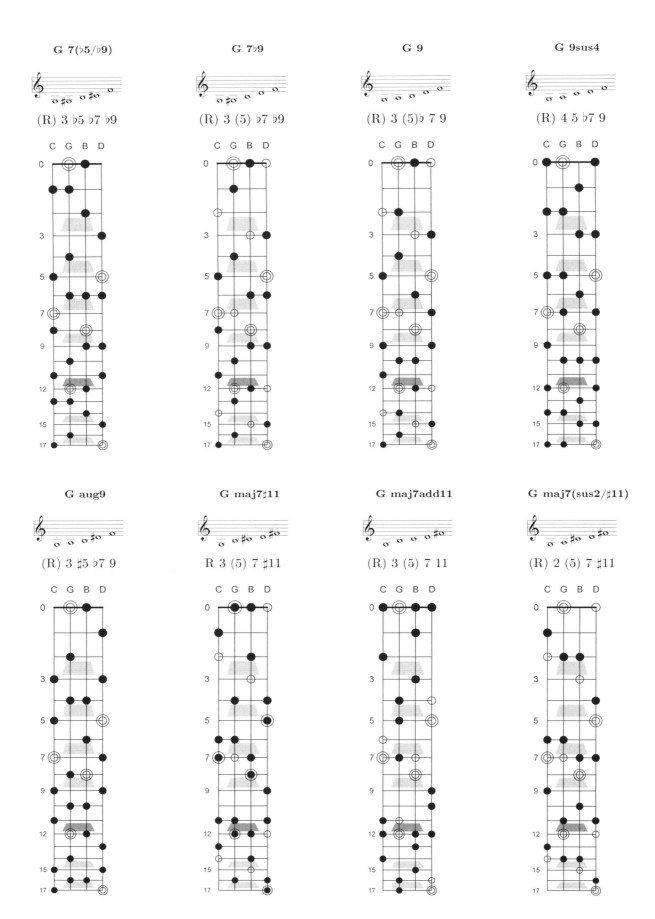

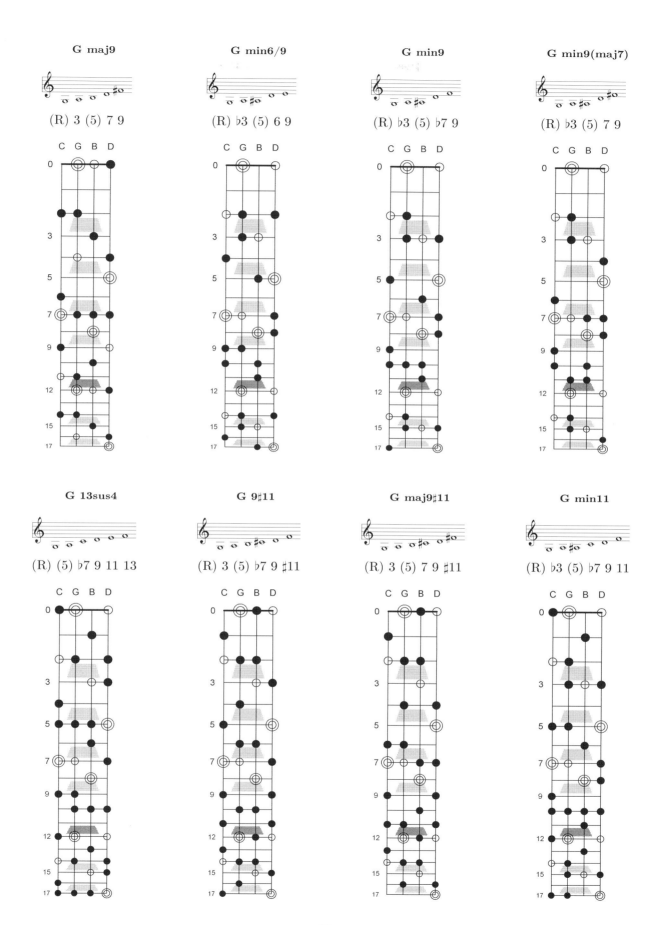

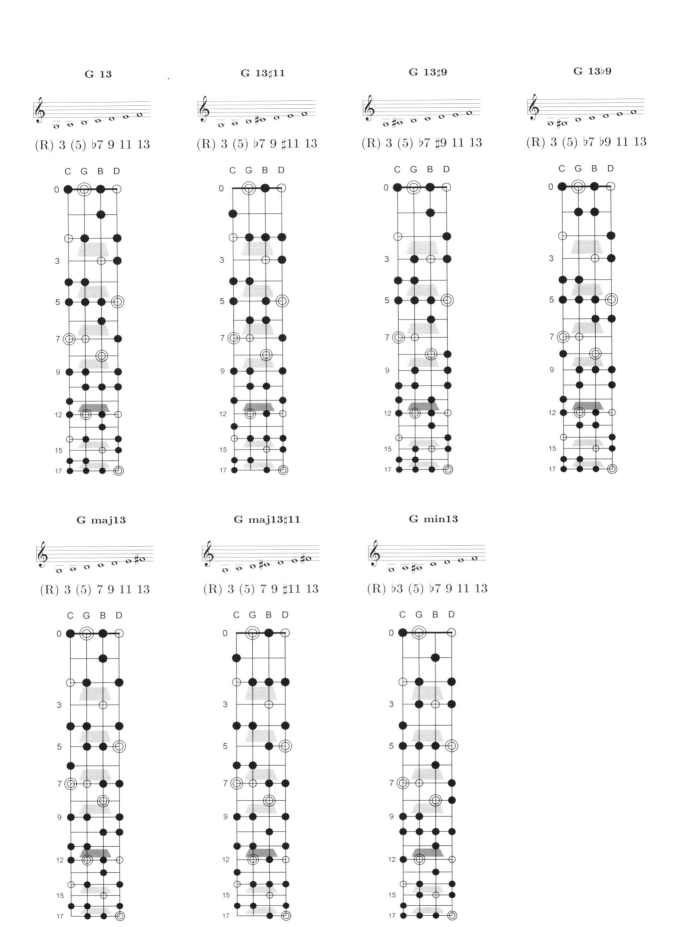

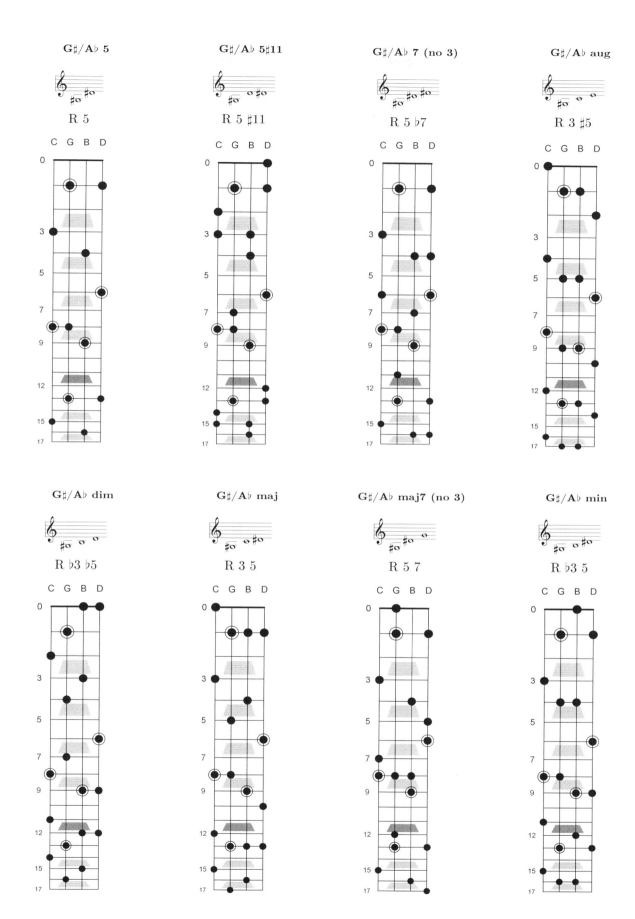

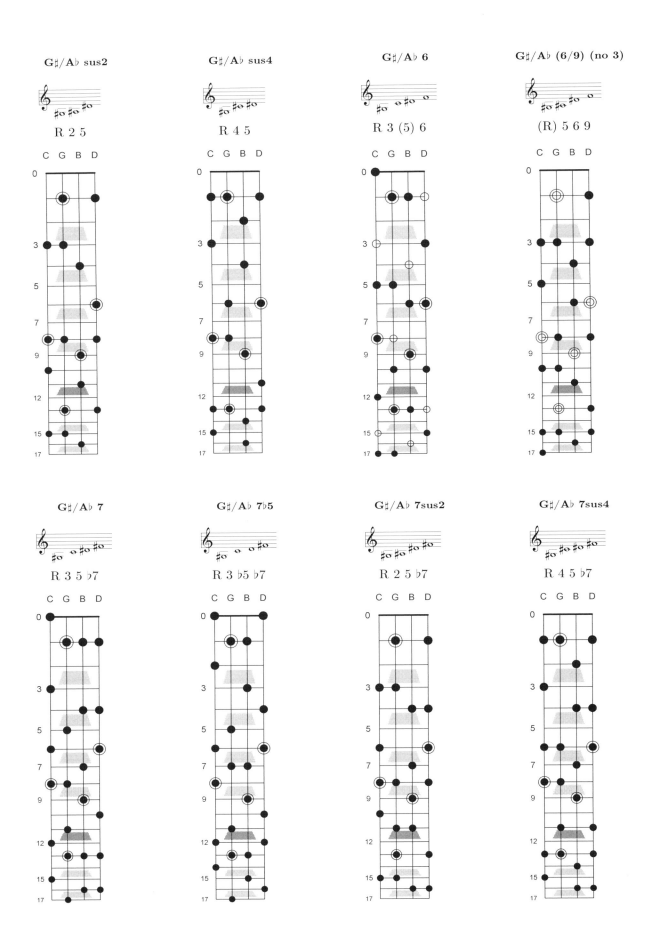

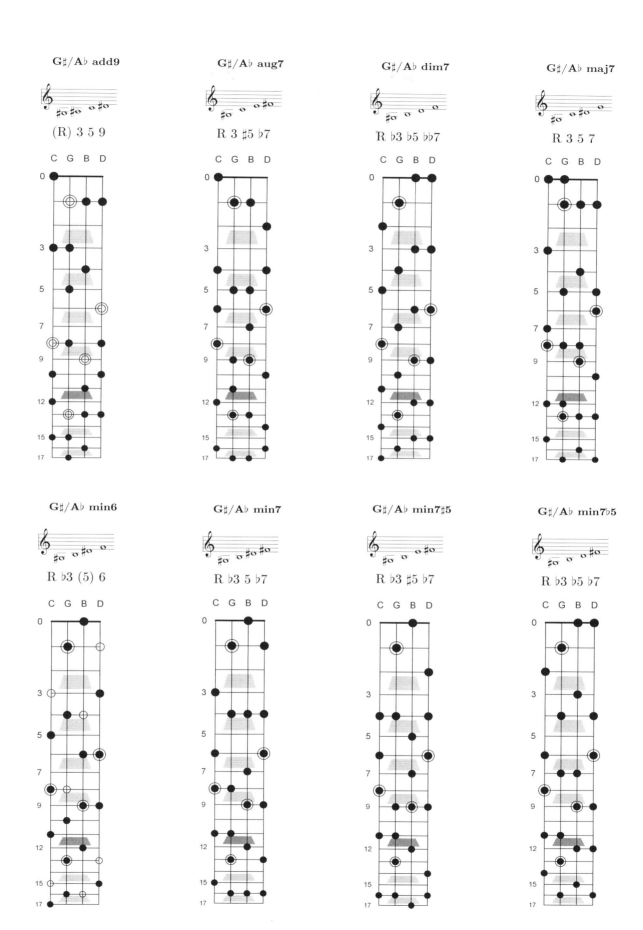

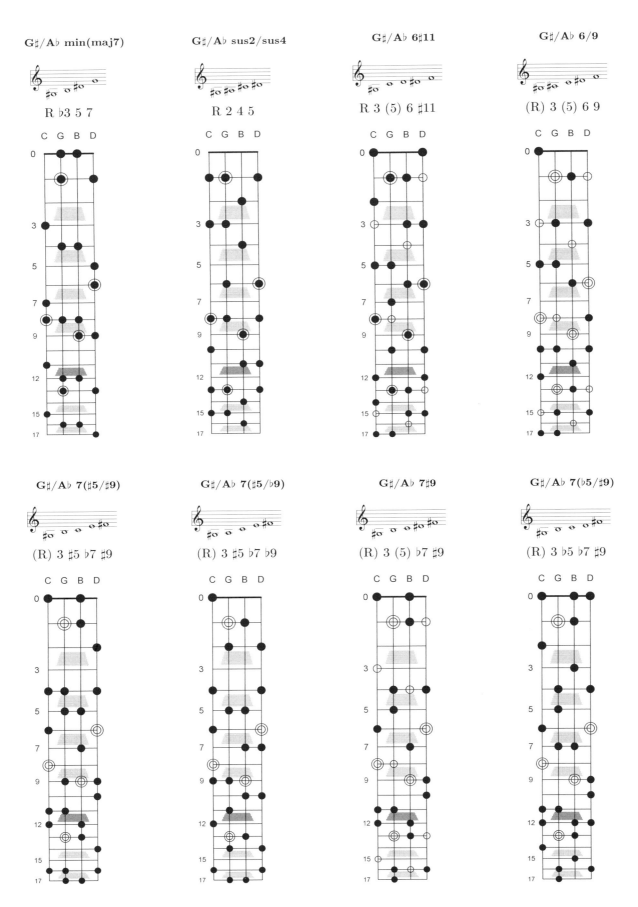

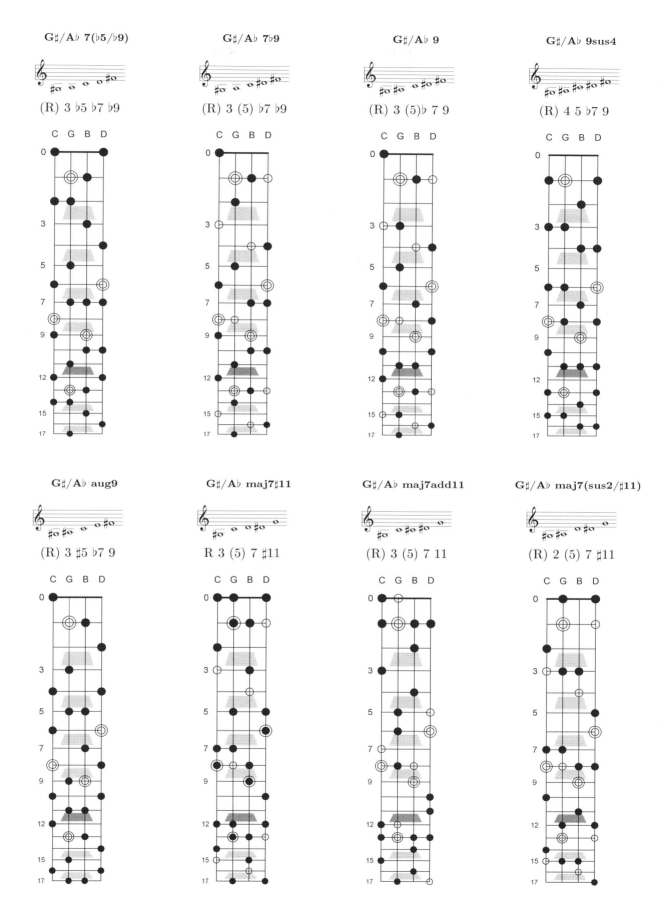

75

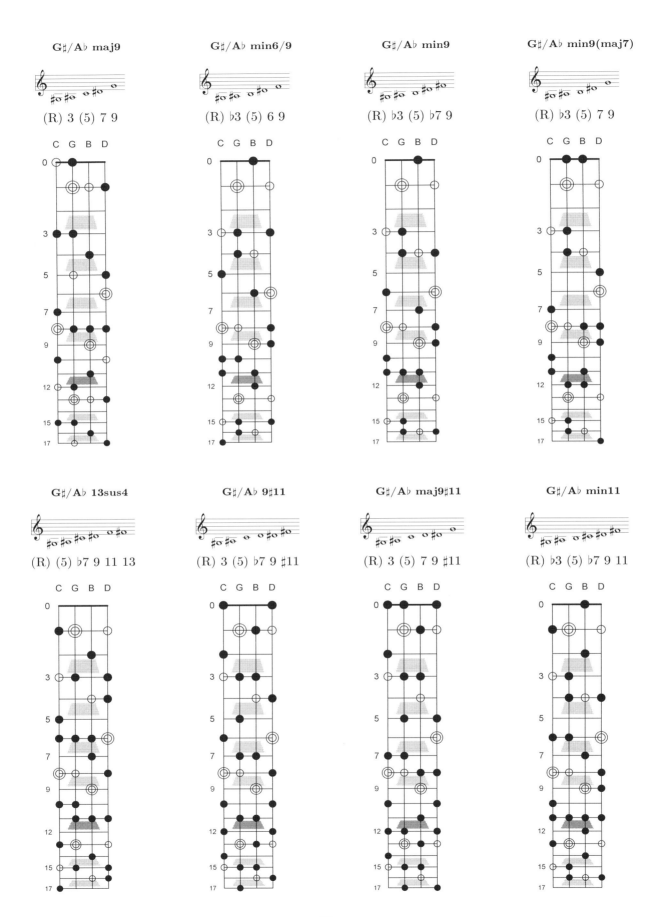

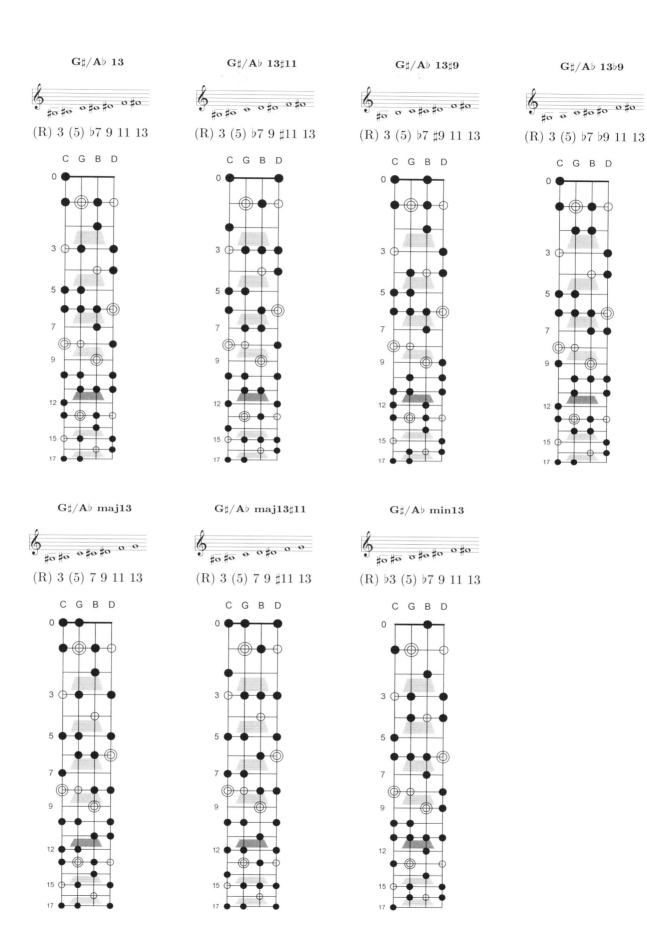

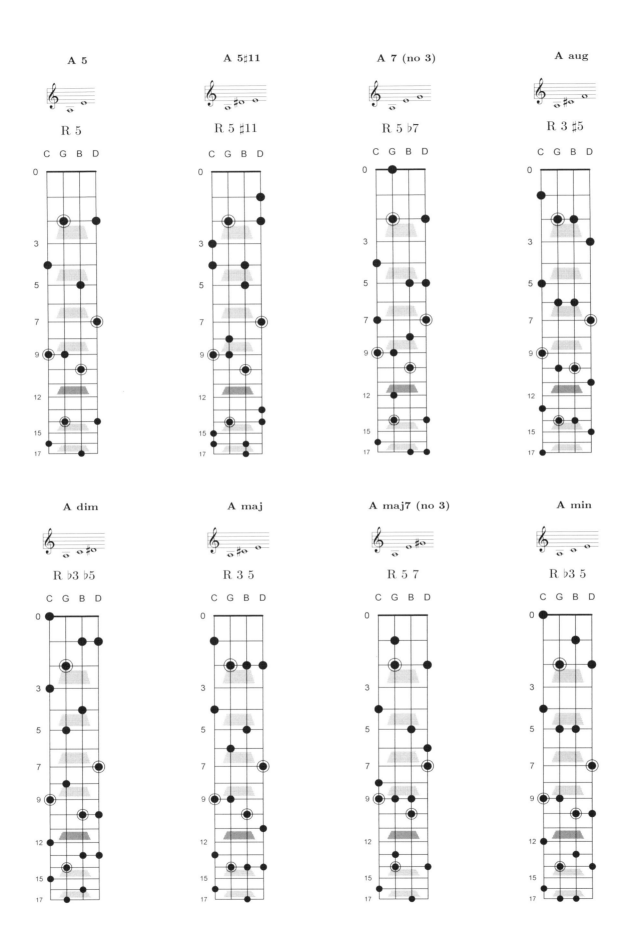

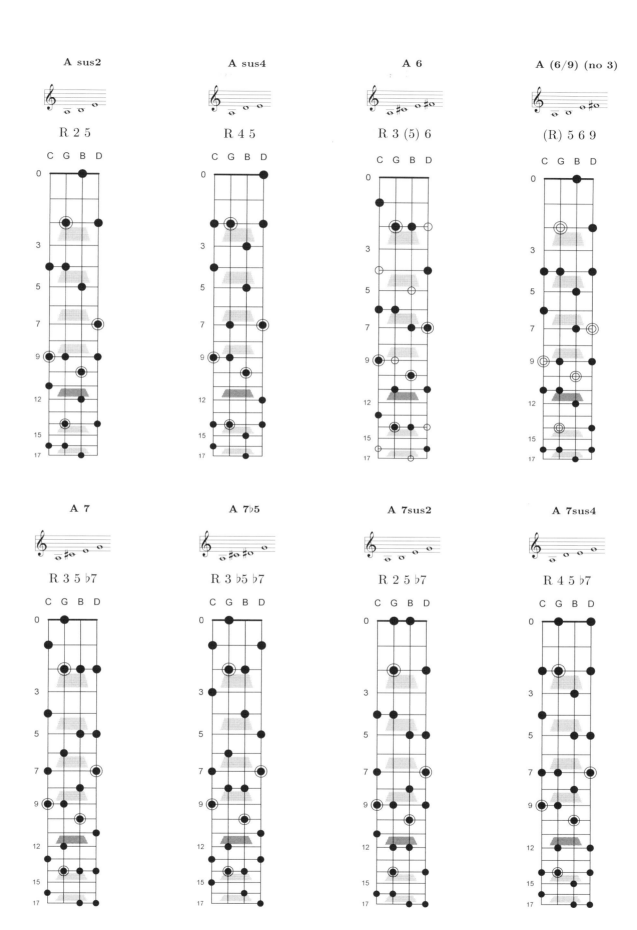

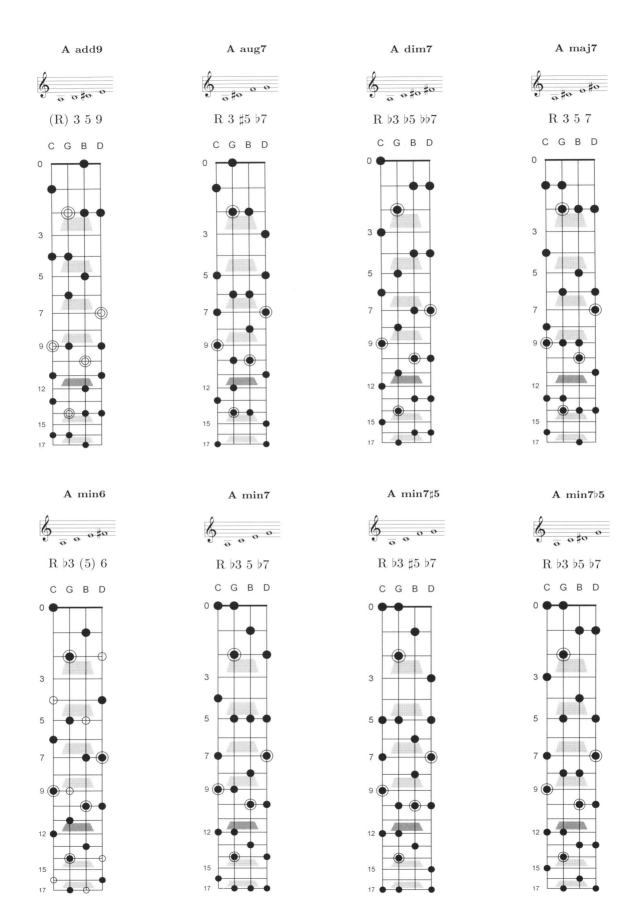

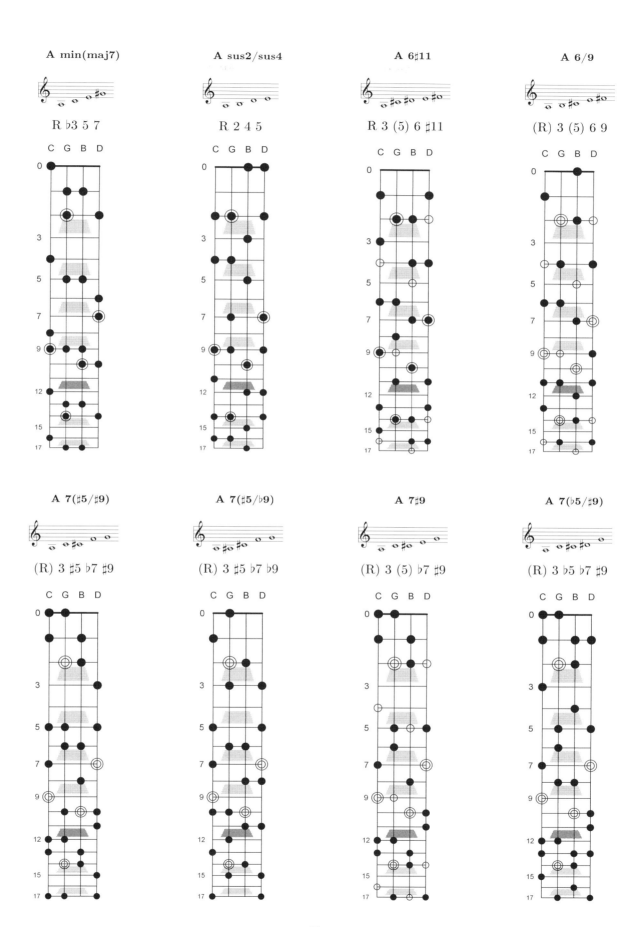

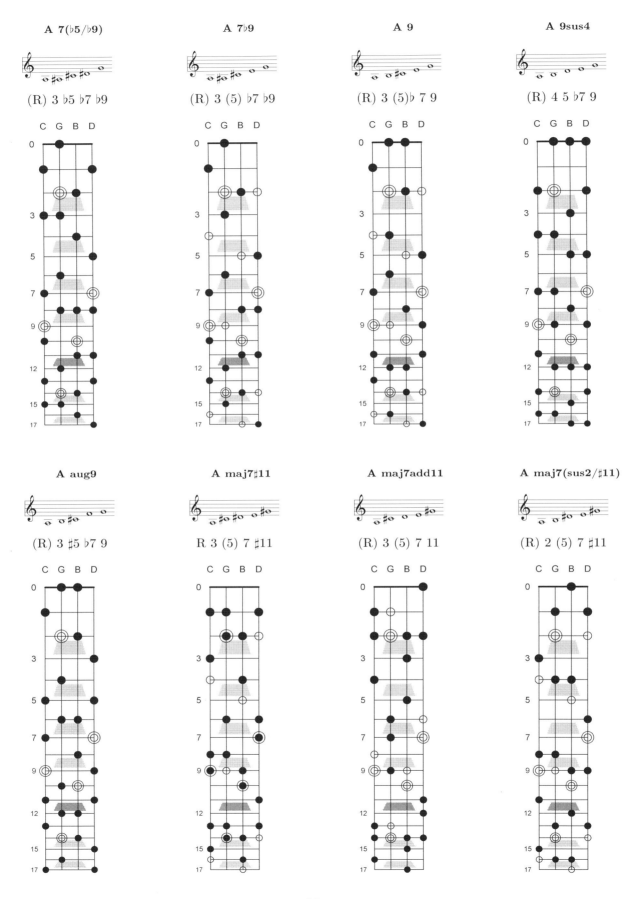

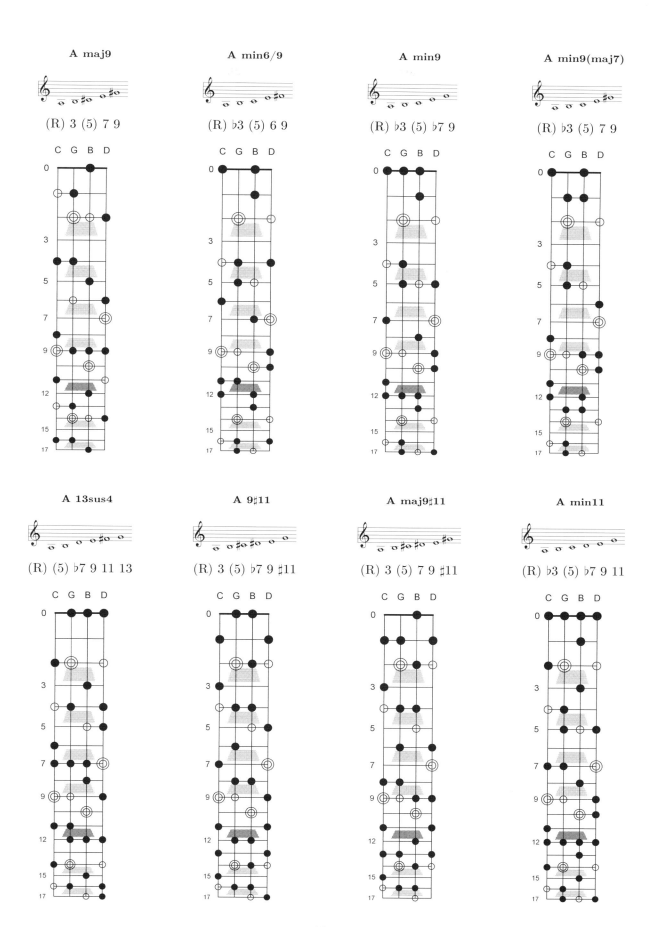

83

A 13

(R) 3 (5) ♭7 9 11 13

A 13♯11

(R) 3 (5) ♭7 9 ♯11 13

A 13♯9

(R) 3 (5) ♭7 ♯9 11 13

A 13♭9

(R) 3 (5) ♭7 ♭9 11 13

A maj13

(R) 3 (5) 7 9 11 13

A maj13♯11

(R) 3 (5) 7 9 ♯11 13

A min13

(R) ♭3 (5) ♭7 9 11 13

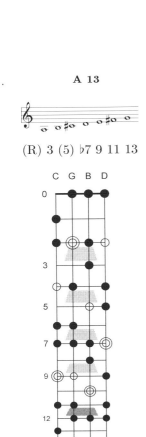
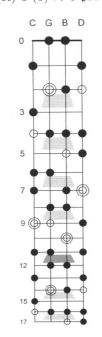
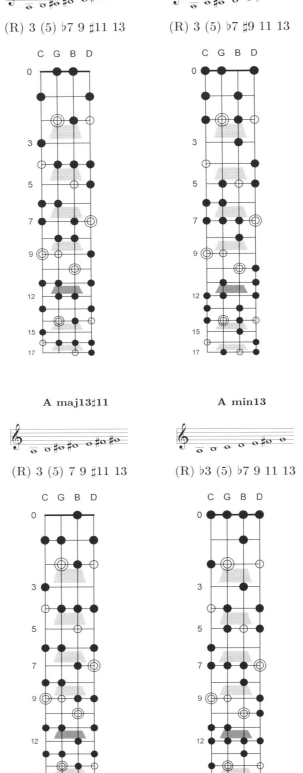
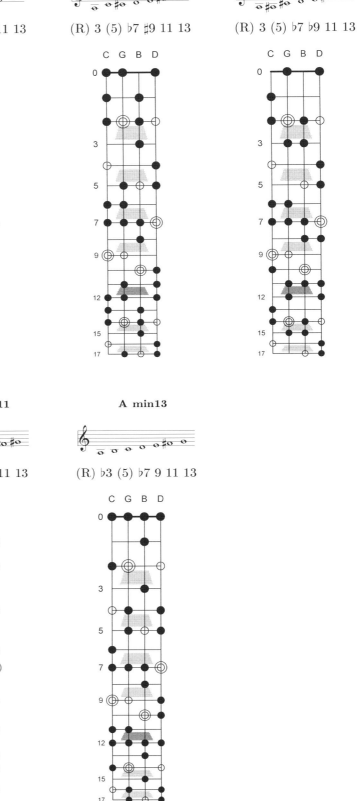

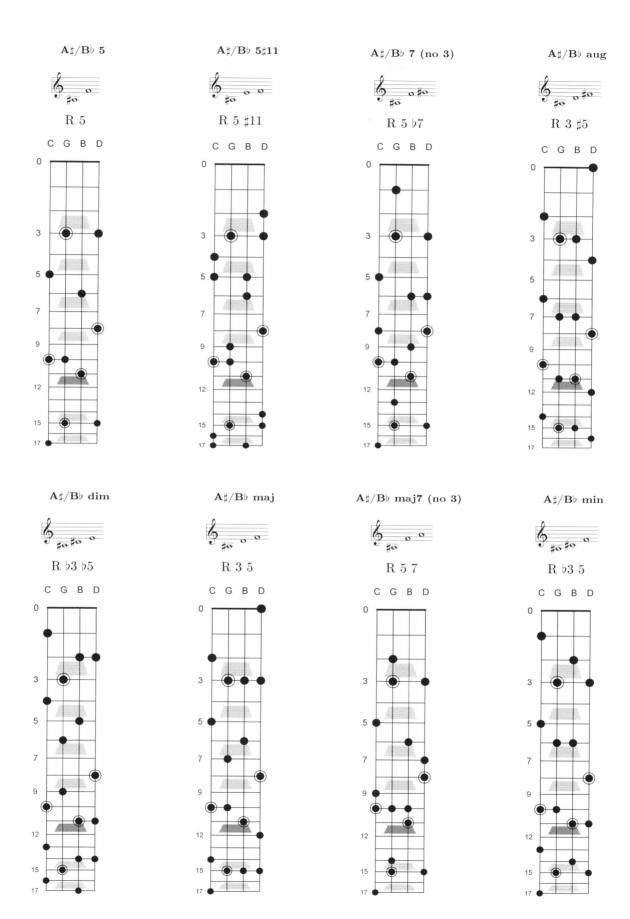

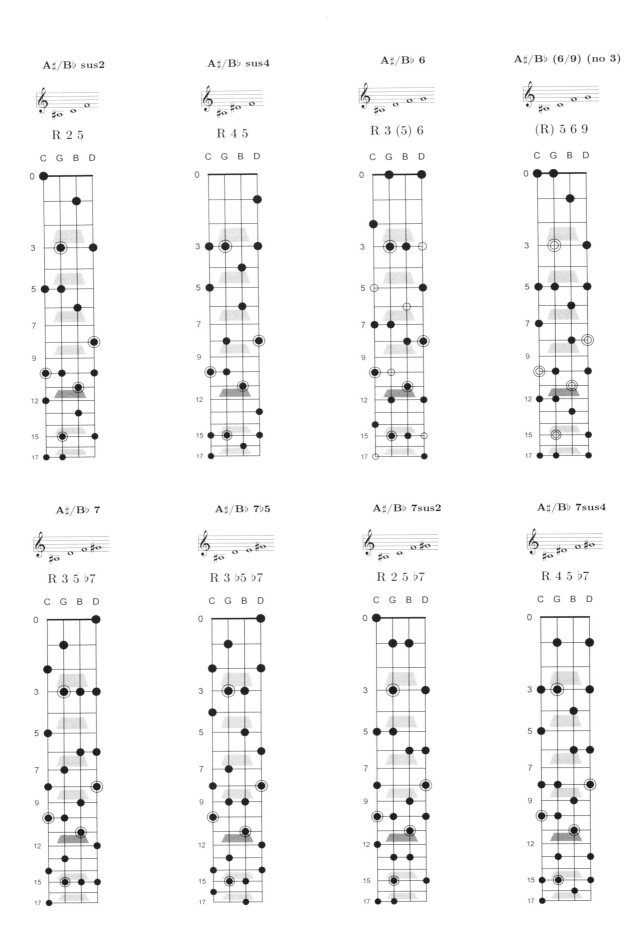

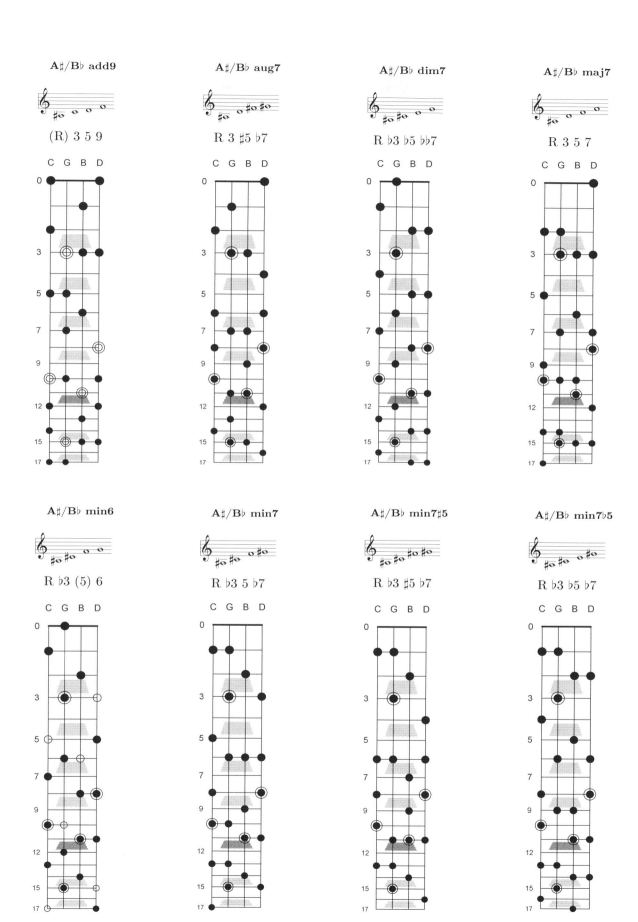

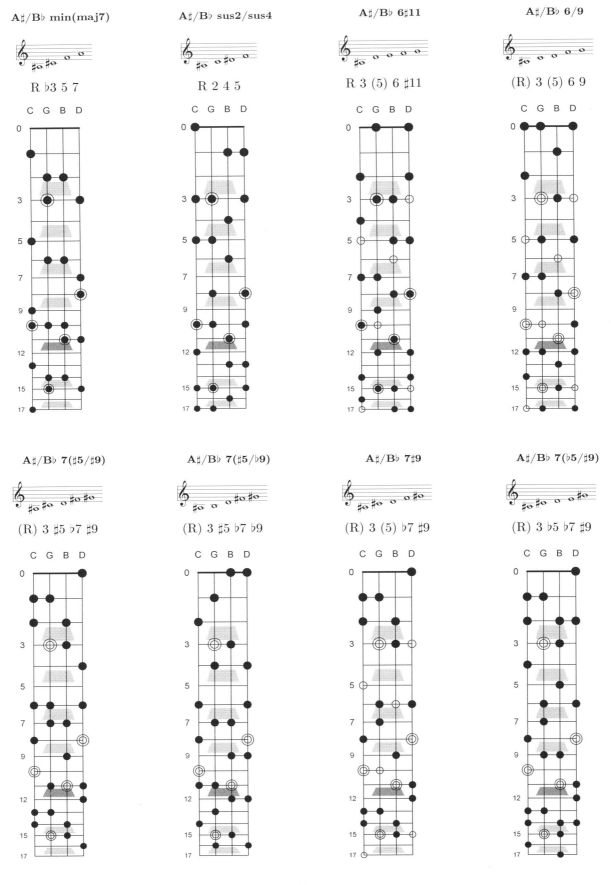

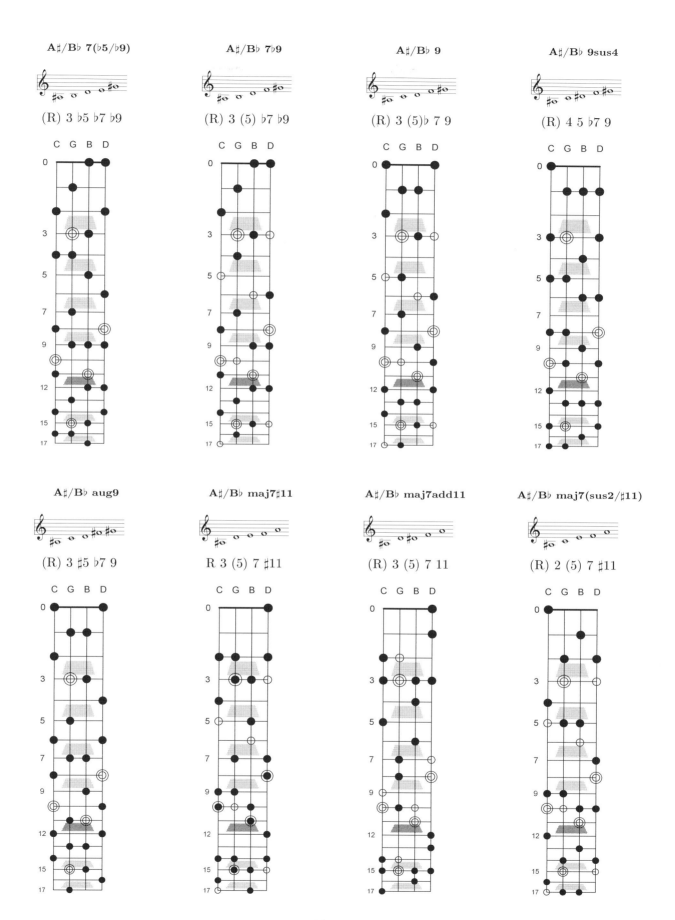

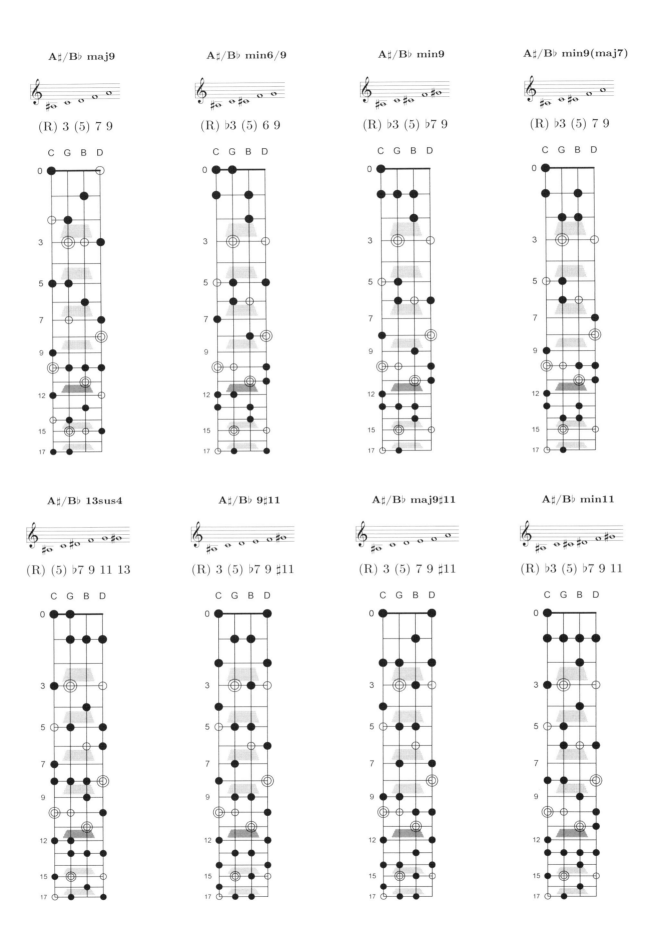

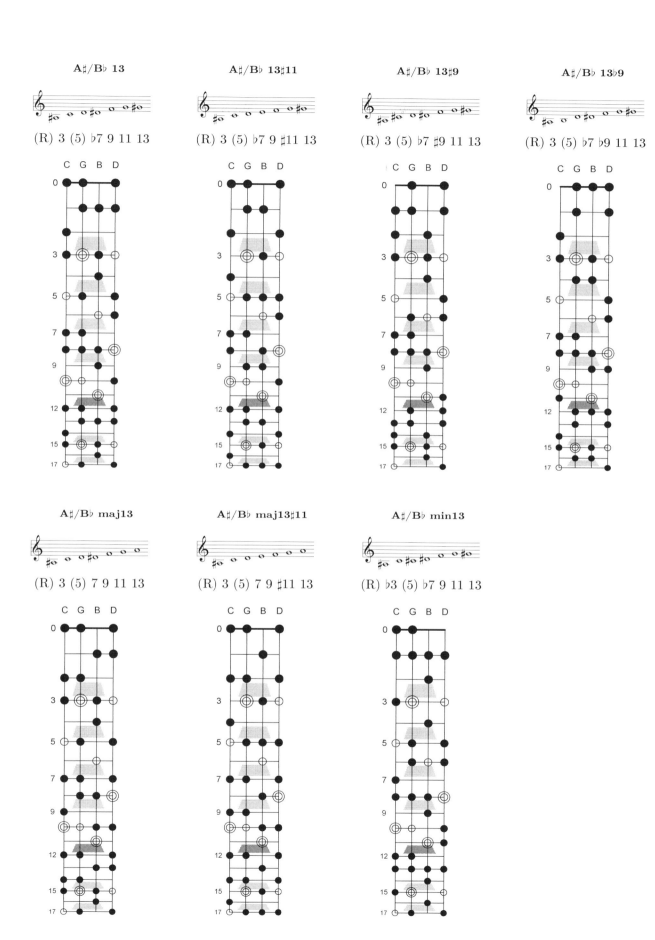

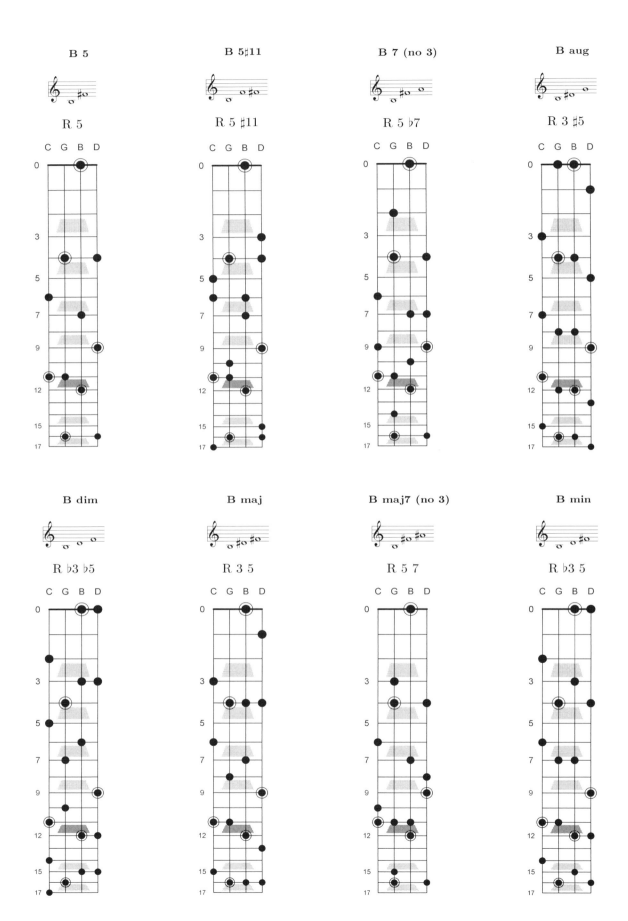

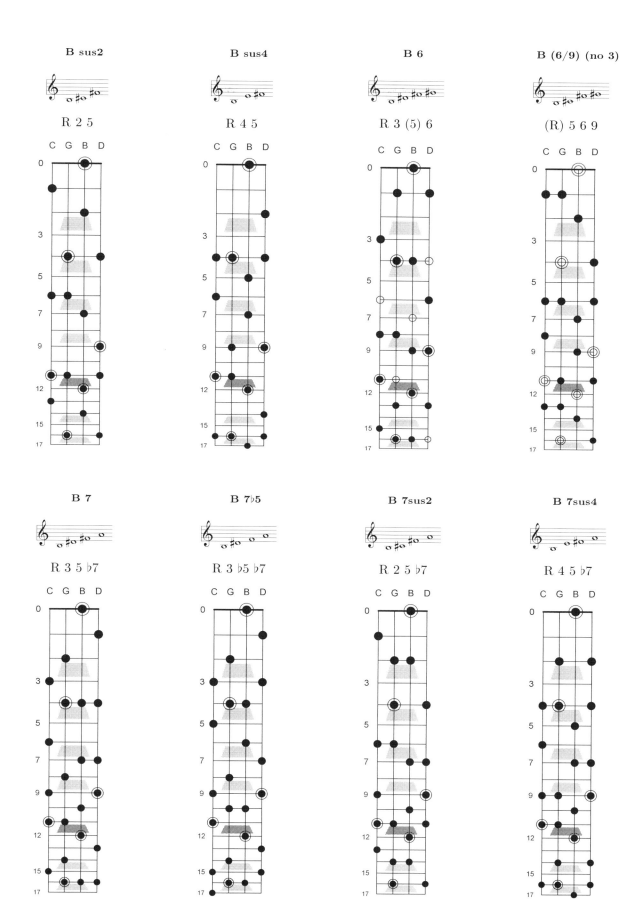

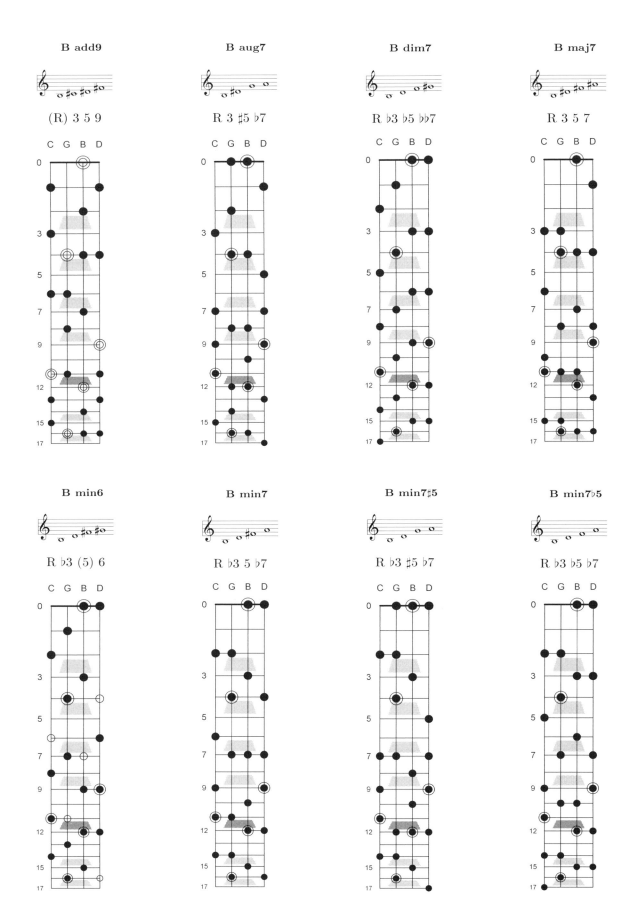

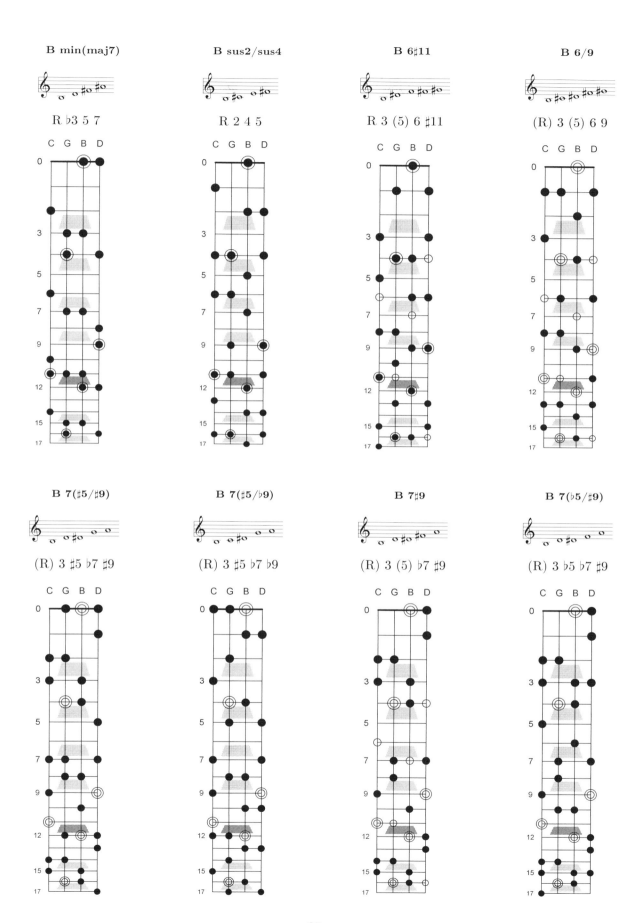

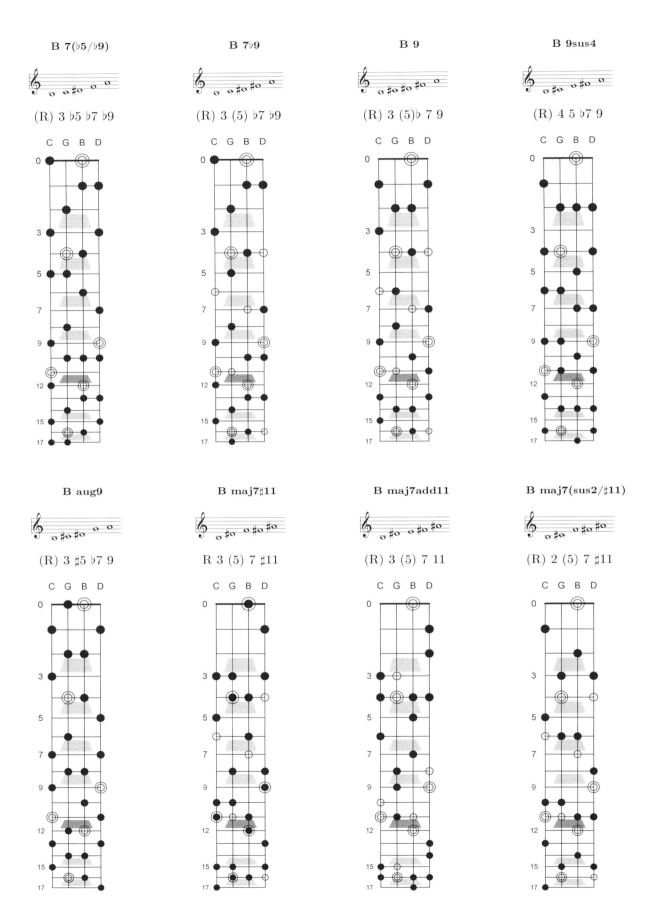

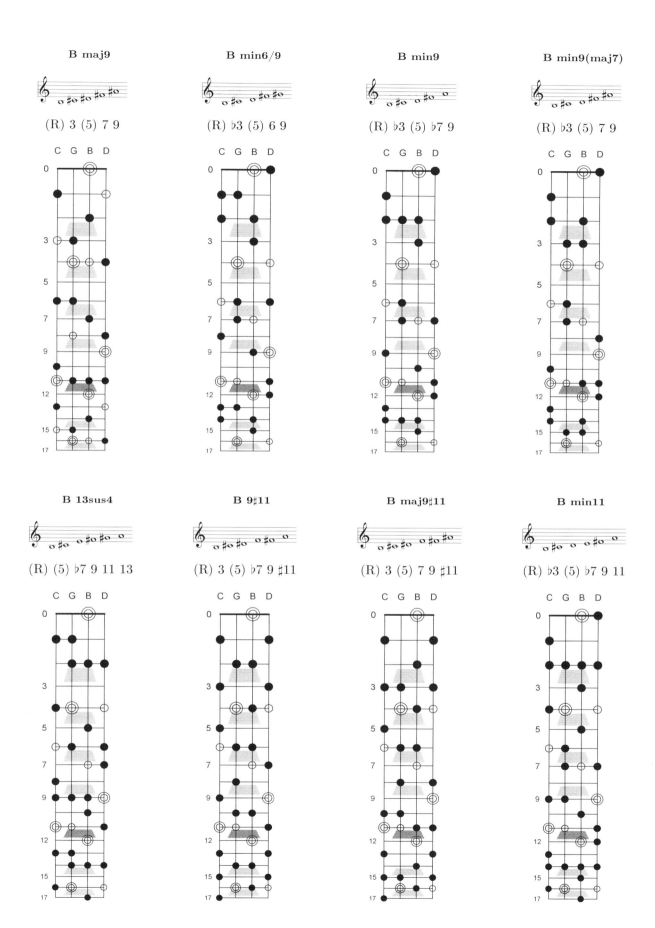

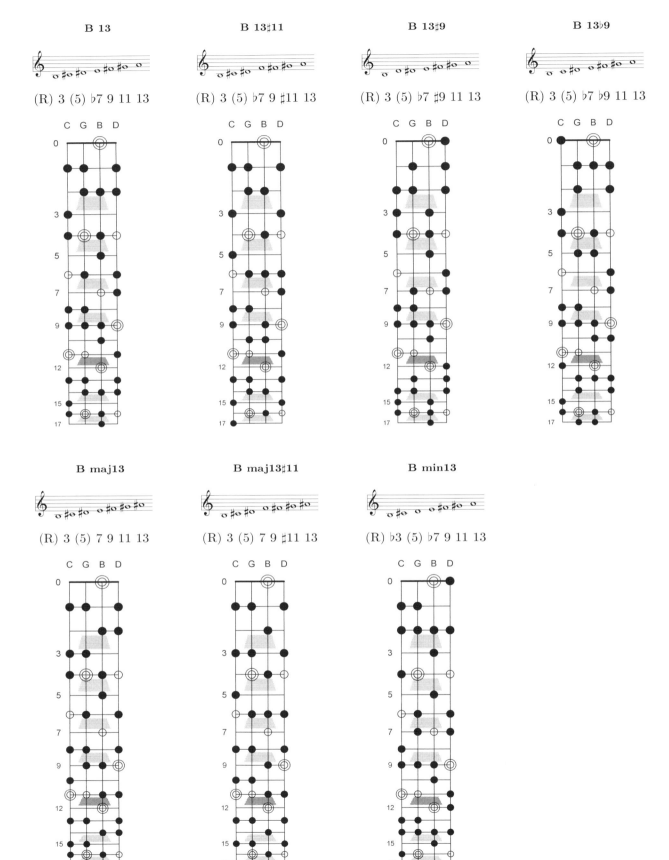

Made in the USA
San Bernardino, CA
04 January 2019